Dedication

Warren dedicates this book to his son Freddie and partner Jane.
Gerry dedicates this book to Hedge.

CONTENTS

IDEAS: 220 PRACTICAL TEACHING IDEAS TO FOSTER ENGAGEMENT AND MOTIVATION IN TEENAGE LEARNERS

Chapter 4

Chapter 5

Chapter 6

Chapter 7

Chapter 8

Chapter 9

ABOUT THE AUTHORS

Warren Kidd is Senior Lecturer and Teaching Fellow at the Cass School of Education, University of East London, where he is the School's Leader in Learning and Teaching. In 2011 Warren was awarded a Teaching Fellowship at the University. Previously, he has taught both sociology and psychology for 14 years in secondary schools and sixth form colleges in Surrey, Kent and London. Along with Gerry, Warren is an experienced author of sociology textbooks aimed at the A level market. For the past 10 years, Warren has worked in the multicultural, urban environment of Newham in east London in the post-compulsory sector as a teacher of sociology, social science manager of a large sixth form college and as a cross-college manager responsible for teaching and learning. In 2007 he completed managing a 'highly commended' Beacon Award action research project in transferable teaching skills. He was the teaching and learning development manager of a large, diverse sixth form college, and was an Advanced Teaching Practitioner.

Gerry Czerniawski is Senior Lecturer in Secondary Social Science and Humanities Education at the Cass School of Education, University of East London. Gerry has passionately worked in the multicultural environment in the London Borough of Newham for over 10 years teaching humanities, sociology and business studies at secondary and post-16 levels before gradually moving into teaching political sciences and education in the higher education sector (The Open University, University of Northampton, London Metropolitan University and London University's Institute of Education). An established author and teacher educator, Gerry still teaches part-time in a comprehensive school in Hertfordshire.

Warren and Gerry are the authors of the 2010 Sage text *Successful Teaching 14–19: Theory, Practice and Reflection*.

ACKNOWLEDGEMENTS

To our colleagues in the Cass School of Education and our trainee teachers who have been the inspiration for this book. Gerry would like to acknowledge Jenny Barksfield, Sarah Meredith, Erica Cattle, Chris Dalladay, John Clarke and Su Garlick for their advice and guidance during the early stages of writing the book. Warren would like to acknowledge Jean Murray for her enthusiasm and support with changing professional identities and roles. Both authors would like to thank Jude Bowen at SAGE for the opportunity to write this text, and for her continued support and guidance. Finally, Warren and Gerry would like to thank Ann Slater, Dean of the Cass School of Education, University of East London, for her continued support and guidance.

FIGURES

HOW TO USE THIS BOOK

What do learners need from us?

Stepping into the classroom is an often exciting, confusing and bewildering social encounter. So many variables can affect what we can and cannot choose to do, and the outcomes that are produced. Above all else, teaching and learning are social encounters. This 'social' context for teaching and learning is true in a number of senses: teaching and learning often require interaction; they are based upon multiple relations with all the history, biography and 'baggage' that affect classroom interaction between teachers and learners; teaching and the classroom experience is often characterized by a wide gambit and roller-coaster of emotional elements, such as compassion, enjoyment, anxiety and support; and learning often takes places within spaces that are highly organized through the roles and scripts of those acting out the social encounters (even if these roles are sometimes unspoken). Finally, teaching and learning (if inside the classroom or in an educational institution) occurs within the context of a broader social community, with all that means for relationships, hierarchies and interaction.

The great social encounter that is classroom teaching

We have written this book with the social encounters between learners and teachers fully in mind. We feel, through years of classroom practice and higher education (HE) teacher education and training, that 'good teaching' and good learning' need to tap into effective and productive relationships and dynamics between those involved. We might refer to this as the 'ethos' of the educational institution or the 'learning atmosphere' or 'climate' of the classroom. We feel that building the right climate is essential for learner motivation and engagement.

Educational change

With changes taking place across the curriculum many established teachers in both school and college environments are now finding themselves facing new, different types of learners than they have previously. Some schools are buying into vocational programmes more than ever before and some colleges are now teaching much younger learners as part of their partnership with local schools. We feel – from the research literature and our own professional roles as teacher educators across a wide variety of programmes – that many teachers feel concerned about the proposition of teaching younger or older learners and often feel ill-equipped with the necessary tools. Having said this, it is also the case that all teachers (new and experienced alike) find adding new ideas to their repertoire and toolbox from time to time a valuable exercise. The trick is to know where to go to get the practical suggestions you might need. This is the motivation behind why we have written this book – to provide ideas that work; ideas we think are worth experimenting with.

The importance of learner motivation

One of the key challenges we hear from many teachers is the perceived difficulty and huge importance of keeping learners interested and engaged. To this end, this book deals with the interrelated issues of:

- motivation;
- challenging all learners across the skills/ability spectrum;
- classroom ethos and management;
- enabling learners to understand their own learning;
- teaching in an exciting, stimulating and engaging way.

We have come to the realization, too, that some trainee teachers and prospective applicants to training programmes often make assumptions about both the behaviour and motivation of young people. We understand the need to 'capture the imagination and creativity of young people' and help enable them to learn to succeed (and to succeed to learn); we understand the central role that motivation and engagement in the learning process plays for successful classroom teaching and learning.

In this book, we intend to speak directly to you, the professional reader, seeking to write a handbook or 'toolbox' of practical suggestions of direct value for classroom teachers new and experienced alike.

Using this book to build your own toolbox

We use the metaphor of the toolbox quite deliberately for this handbook because:

- we have found it useful to see teachers as 'crafts persons' building a repertoire of skills and practices;
- we see teaching and learning in the classroom as fundamentally shaped by the quality of the relationships between all those involved – relationships which can be very effectively shaped by the ideas and solutions in the book;
- we see teachers (new and experienced) needing to reflect upon their practice and adding and updating their toolbox from time to time to ensure the greatest and most effective range of skills and teaching techniques as possible;
- we think that it is useful to focus upon teaching as a 'practical doing' which needs to be both scripted and spontaneous, and learning as needing to be orchestrated and managed as well as open and creative.

The handbook or 'toolbox' approach of the text means that:

1. We have written this book deliberately in a tone that starts with the assumption that everyone can learn. We see the job of the teacher to support and enable learners to learn as effectively as possible.
2. We decided to write in a voice that speaks directly to the teacher-as-reader.
3. We also decided to prioritize ideas and suggestions over theoretical discussion, although everything we write has been informed 'in the background' by research and theory at every stage.
4. The book is structured so that each chapter starts with a list of 'problems to be solved' – key issues and challenges that are faced by the classroom practitioner and which are directly addressed by the ideas within each chapter. We conclude each chapter with questions for your own professional development: questions posed to you, our readers, asking you to reflect on things you have tried, to see if and how they worked and why.
5. Each practical idea you will encounter in this book is both 'named and numbered' – the book as a whole building up to a large list of techniques that constitutes the 'toolbox' we have referred to in the title.

Ethos

We feel that a great deal of student motivation and the creation of a positive learning atmosphere comes down to the ethos all participants build into learning processes and learning encounters. Equally, this book – a guide to practitioners – also has its own ethos or 'spirit' comprised of the following three elements:

- **practical teaching ideas** – aimed at supporting teachers with the difficult and essential task of motivating and supporting learners;
- A sense of a **handbook** to be used to navigate the reader's way through practical teaching ideas;
- A **trouble-shooting approach**: each chapter identifies problems, challenges and scenarios and then offers advice on how to deal with these problems with concrete ideas and recommendations.

The spirit of this handbook is 'this is what works'; the book offers practical ideas covering the themes of:

- classroom activities;
- ideas for assessment which motivate and engage;
- use of group work for learner engagement;
- using e-learning strategies;
- ways of organizing the teaching space;
- classroom management and behavioural management and their differences;
- setting learning atmospheres and ethos;
- rewarding learning;
- stretching the more able;
- rule setting;
- developing learners' meta-cognition;
- capturing and utilizing the learner voice;
- developing independent learning skills.

For a complete list of all the ideas contained in this book see the list starting on page x.

Features of the text

1. Each chapter starts with the chapter overview – a list of five or six 'problem-solving issues' for the reader for each chapter. We then draw upon these issues throughout the chapter and provide ideas which you can add to your toolbox as a means to help 'solve' these initial challenges.

We then go back to these issues at the end and ask you, once you have experimented with some of the tools, to reflect upon their successfulness as a matter for your own professional development.

2. Leading on from the chapter overview we provide a 'context' for why these issues matter and how they might link to and affect student motivation and engagement. We have also contextualized our practical ideas and offer them to you 'grounded' and weighted in research evidence where possible.

3. The majority of each chapter takes the shape of a list of ideas and strategies for you to experiment with.

4. Each chapter ends with a 'checklist' with a list of important principles for you to remember when building your own 'toolbox'.

Throughout the text you will see two helpful boxes: **Reflection point** – these are questions posed to you to help contextualize the ideas you are reading about and to aid you in applying them to your own practice; and **Best practice** – a list of bullet points summarizing key practice in this aspect of teaching and learning.

We hope you enjoy this book and, perhaps more importantly, we hope that you and your learners enjoy the productive teaching and learning that the ideas seek to foster. Remember to come back to the book from time to time, adding layer upon layer of reflection and providing the opportunity for you to 'take stock'. Remember that teachers are learners too – and one of the most useful learning opportunities we can provide is to demonstrate our own learning to those who populate our classrooms.

CHAPTER 1

HOW TO 'SPARKLE' IN THE CLASSROOM

Chapter overview

The aims of the chapter are to:

1. Introduce a variety of strategies managing the entrance of learners to classrooms.
2. Examine a range of starter, plenary and end activities suitable for teenage learners.
3. Explore the use of source materials for stimulating lesson activities.
4. Provide a range of activities that capture and sustain teenage interest in your subject.

Problem-solving

In this chapter, we consider how to capture the interest of a teenage audience in your subject area. As teachers, authors and ex-teenagers, we recognize the difficulties in engaging and sustaining the interest of many young people who find the learning activities they experience in schools and colleges mundane and/or far removed from their own interests and passions. This chapter offers a range of activities designed to ignite the creativity and imagination of teenage learners. We passionately believe that teaching and engaging teenagers is one of the most rewarding and exciting experiences within the teaching profession. We also acknowledge that teenagers can be the most demanding and critical of audiences. But once motivated, these young people can provide never-ending streams of creativity and imagination, and allow the teacher to conduct, rather than dictate, the conditions in which young people learn best. We hope that the ideas in this and the following chapters enable you to become conductor rather than dictator, making you and your subject sparkle in the eyes of teenage learners.

Context

Understanding what we mean by 'motivation' can be problematic. Definitions differ depending on who/what we are trying to motivate (for example, adults/children/animals/individuals/groups), which theories/concepts we are deploying when discussing it (for example, psychological/sociological), and what sort of institution (for example, a school, college or place of work). Some writers argue that adults have four significant reward systems: money, usefulness, status and the gratitude or approval of those we live with (Marland, 1993). However this is of little significance to teenagers where few such rewards are possible within the school or college they attend. Motivation can take many forms. For example it can be 'intrinsic' to the teenager (that is, stems from within via their interests, values, desires, and so on) or 'extrinsic (that is, stems from outside in the variety of ways they can be rewarded, coerced, threatened, and so on). Maslow's (1987) hierarchy of needs (physiological, safety, love and belonging, self-esteem and self-actualization) is a motivational theory in psychology that provides a useful evaluation framework for teachers when reviewing and planning the efficacy of their lessons. His theory argues that while people aim to meet basic needs, they seek to meet successively higher needs in the form of a hierarchy. The implication for teachers is that successful learning can only take place if all of Maslow's 'needs' can be fulfilled by the learner. While there are many other theories that we touch upon elsewhere (Kidd and Czerniawski, 2010) it is worth considering Maslow's theory when thinking about how best to engage and motivate teenage learners.

Toolbox

Managing entrances of learners to classrooms

How often do young people enter classrooms with little sense of purpose, curiosity or excitement? By combining a welcoming environment with a purposeful approach to the facilitation of tasks, teenagers will quickly get the message that not only do you care about them as individuals but that you are also passionate about how much they can achieve in the small amount of time they are with you.

Best practice – entering the classroom

Entering the classroom is a key moment to capture learners right from the start. Practitioners have found it useful to consider:

- Rules for learners outside the classroom (for example, lining up; gender separation; with/without bags, in silence).
- Classroom layout (for example, positioning of tables/workspaces, chairs, desk).
- Classroom environment (for example, lighting, plants, heating, wall displays, music playing in background, ventilation).
- Location of teacher (for example, by the open door greeting students, at the front of classroom ready to issue instructions).
- Starter activity (for example, on desks as students walk in; activity projected on smart board).

 Idea 1.1

Young Sherlock

Get your learners to line up quietly outside the classroom/workshop and tell them there are 10 visible clues placed around the room. Their job is to write down the clues and guess what the topic of the lesson is going to be. Alternatively give them each an envelope with a simple observational task in it (for example, write down 10 items they have seen today related to their subject).

 Idea 1.2

Don't blame the DJ

Raise expectations of what is to come in the lesson by handing each learner an envelope in the corridor with a task in it. Inform them that they must complete the task before the end of the music they hear on entrance to the classroom. The first one to complete the task gets to choose the music played in the next lesson.

Idea 1.3

Total recall

Put a complex picture on the board that relates to the lesson you are about to teach and ask learners to remember as many features as possible from the picture (you could also offer a 'prize' for the best memory). Remove the picture and get learners in 2 minutes of silence to write down as many elements of the picture that they can recall. Use these elements to launch your lesson.

Best practice – first impressions

Practitioners have found it effective to consider:

- The importance of 'first impressions', that is, warm greetings from teacher to learners, classroom layout, quality of resources, room lighting, and so on.
- Familiarity with classroom equipment, for example, knowing how to turn on/off video/DVD/audio equipment, ease of use with all elements of information and communication technology (ICT) and so on.
- The importance of eye contact, physical posture and body language when teaching.
- The balance between classroom persona and corridor persona, that is, the importance in engaging students out of the classroom in a friendly and enthusiastic way regardless of what may/may not have happened in class.

 Idea 1.4

Mini-whiteboard magic!

Make in advance a class set of mini-whiteboards (laminate A4 white card, place this in a wallet and add a marker pen). Have these on the tables as learners enter your classroom. Get them to draw a pictorial representation of a key concept related to your subject. The person sitting next to them then has to guess what that key concept is.

 **Idea 1.5**

Sorted!

Immediately establish competition as an element of your classroom practice by placing a 'group performance chart' on the wall of your classroom. Split the class into groups of four or five students, giving each group a specific table to sit at. In some of your lessons start off by giving each group a task in an envelope (for example, organizing cards in order of significance; chronological order; theoretical similarity). The first group to correctly complete the task gets a star placed on their performance chart. The group that progresses furthest by half-term wins a prize from you.

Exciting ways to start lessons

Have you ever stopped to wonder how many classes start in exactly the same way? Learners copy down aims and objectives, teachers call out the register, learners are given any important notices, and so on. Is it any wonder that some young people are not 'bovvered' about turning up for the first few mintues of a lesson, that is, they know there will be nothing particularly special that they have missed. Successful motivation will have your learners rushing to your lesson in the belief that they might be missing something special. Starts to all of your lessons need to capture learners' imaginations and set up high expectations for teachers and learners alike. The following ideas should help you achieve this.

 Idea 1.6

Google Earth tour

You will need computers in your classroom for this but it's worth it! Using Google Earth/Street tour, get learners in pairs or threes to carry out an 'e' expedition somewhere where they might never have been (for example, the forests of Borneo, the inner-slums of Mexico). Get each group to work on a different theme/destination/concept depending on what is appropriate for your subject. Learners report back to the class what the outcomes were. This works beautifully as both a starter and a main class activity.

Idea 1.7
Quiz ball

A fun way to start lessons and get everyone on board: buy a juggling ball (or scrunch up a piece of paper) and throw it to a learner, asking them a question related to the lesson you previously taught. If/when they answer the question correctly they can throw the ball to another classmate and ask them a new question, and so on. This helps create a really snappy pace at the start – essential for those 'sparkling' learning atmospheres.

Idea 1.8
Question master

Each learner is asked to write down, in complete silence, five questions related to the previous lesson to which they know the answers. They can use their notes/books and so on, but they must know the answers. They can then either test each other in their pairs/groups or you can choose one group to randomly fire questions at other class members (you can always choose a different group each week). Make this more fun by getting them to pretend there is an imaginary buzzer which they must hit before answering.

Idea 1.9
Jigsaw puzzle

Make a quick jigsaw puzzle (simply cut up laminated images from magazines/newspapers or photocopied from your textbook). Provide each group/pair with a set and get learners to complete this as quickly as possible. Make sure that the completed image contains within it key concepts associated with your subject. Learners then have to guess what the concepts are and/or what the theme of today's lesson is.

Idea 1.10

Diamond-9

This tried and tested starter is easy to re-create. Using Word or Publisher on your computer, create nine squares that can fit together in the shape of a diamond. In each square produce a contestable statement. Laminate each set and place in an envelope. Learners in pairs or groups of three are asked to rank statements in a diamond shape according to if they agree/disagree with them.

Plenaries and ends to lessons

What is the difference between activities described as 'plenaries' and those described as 'ends'? Quite often a plenary can be the opportunity to summarize, recap or evaluate a particular section of your lesson before moving on to the next phase of the lesson. This means that they are more than just joins between activities but, rather, activities in their own right. 'Ends' are 'plenaries' that come at the end of a lesson and are an opportunity for teachers to evaluate how successfully the aims and objectives of the lesson have been met. Plenaries can actually occur at any time in the lesson – and usually follow on from a task before the class moves on to something else. In this way plenaries are recaps that help aid transitions in your sequences of events. The following activities can be used for both 'plenaries' and 'ends'.

Reflection point

Remember – plenaries are themselves *reflection points* for learners and teachers alike! These key moments distil learning and offer the opportunity for learners to 'take stock' and crystallize the learning journey. Plenaries offer teachers key opportunities to receive feedback on learning, to assess learning and to provide clarity on future instructions, direction and facilitation. Plenaries, therefore, through engaging learners in reflection, enable teachers and learners to connect the various segments of the lesson together in one continuous story.

Idea 1.11
Speed dating

Arrange the room in the fashion of a speed-dating scenario, that is, one long line of tables with chairs arranged so that two people will always be seated opposite each other. Make sure that you have five or six themes that you wish learners to discuss. Call out the first theme and give the class two minutes to discuss before blowing a whistle. Keep one side of the class seated in the same seats but make sure all the others move down one person. Launch your second theme and continue until you have used all your themes.

 Idea 1.12
Mad Hatter

Ask learners to write one question on a piece of paper and scrunch it up, putting it into a hat that you have brought to the lesson. Shake the hat around and then ask each student to take one question out of the hat. Each has to read out the question and answer it.

 Idea 1.13
Last one standing

All members of the class stand up. Each learner has to think of one fact they have learnt in the lesson and after successfully telling the class they can then sit down (or leave the class, depending on if plenary or end).

 Idea 1.14
Don't mention it

Learners choose, from a bag, a term they have learnt during the lesson. They should attempt to describe, in a maximum of 30 seconds, the term to the other members of the class without using the word itself. Learners put their hand up as soon as they know the answer.

Best practice – that personal touch!

Practitioners have found it effective to consider:

- How important it is to remember a particular hobby or interest that a learner may have. This offers invaluable opportunities as learners enter your class (or as you pass them in the corridor) to enquire after their interest, raising their esteem before your lesson starts.
- The importance of lighting and ventilation during any lesson. Classrooms need to be well lit and airy places for attention spans to be maximized.
- The importance of use of names. Try to avoid referring to a class as 'year 9s' and, whenever possible, use learners' first names. This is a powerful classroom management tool and makes pupils feel that you are interested in them and not just your subject.
- The importance of having a task on the board or the tables as learners enter the classroom as a way of immediately engaging them in your lesson.

 Idea 1.15

Who am I?

Split the class into groups of four or five learners. Each group is given a set of Post-it notes. Each member of the group writes the name of a famous person related to the subject taught and sticks it on the forehead of the person next to them. That group member is allowed up to 20 questions to find out the name of the person stuck to their head.

 Idea 1.16

Cubism?

Create or get hold of a large cube or very large dice that you can write on. On each side write a generic question (for example, one thing I learnt today? One key concept I learnt today?). Create enough die for each group. Let the members of the group roll the dice in turn and answer the questions.

Using source materials for stimulating activities

To what extent does your subject rely on the ability of learners to work with sources (for example, photographs, statistics, diary extracts, letters)? All too often, many learners have little opportunity to develop the range of skills required for examiners to award the maximum marks available. Using a variety of different sources can make subjects come alive to students, motivating them in your subject. The following ideas offer suggestions as to how this might be achieved.

Idea 1.17

Chain of events

Split the class into groups giving each group a separate image to look at. Groups decide what led up to and what follows the particular event depicted in the picture. This can be written down or fed back to the class as a whole. A variation of this can be done by stopping a DVD at a particular point and asking each group to predict what happens next.

Idea 1.18

Speech bubbles

As with Idea 1.17 above, each group is given an image to look at but with people present in each photograph. Prepare some blank speech bubbles (you can laminate both the picture and the bubbles) and get each group to write appropriate quotations in the bubbles and place them on the photographs. Each group then reads out their comments to the class, justifying why they have chosen those words.

Best practice – sparkling in the classroom

When trying to be a dynamic classroom performer providing a sparkling classroom atmosphere, you should consider:

- The energy and enthusiasm that you convey about your subject and your learners.
- The impact of the classroom environment that learners walk into.
- How up to date you are with recent developments in your subject area/s.
- How you make your subject relevant to lives of teenage learners.
- How approachable you are to learners facing difficulties with your subject.

Idea 1.19
Hold the front page!

Using Publisher, design a mock-up front page for a newspaper and include in it a series of photographs related to your subject but leave blank any copy that might have been inserted. Tell learners that the stories to go with the photographs have been wiped from the computer by accident and that the paper cannot go to print until they write new stories to match the photographs.

Idea 1.20
Foreign correspondent!

Split the class up into groups of four or five learners. On each table provide a range of source-based resources (for example, photographs, letters, newspaper clippings). Each table represents a different country. Each group is to send one of its 'foreign correspondents' to each table and by using 'how, why, where, when, who' they are to return to their group with a story about the country in question. The homework or follow-up activity is to design a mock-up newspaper coverage of the countries being investigated.

Reflection point

To what extent are teachers and their learners restricted by their own 'comfort zones'? Many teachers worry about trying out new ideas with classes they are not used to teaching. Similarly many learners groan when teachers try out new table arrangements, seating strategies or new activities. None of this need worry you if right from the very first lesson you experiment with new ideas that capture and sustain the interest of learners. They will quickly associate your lessons with purposeful learning, fun and curiosity, and will be open to all sorts of ideas. Stay with habit and your ability to bring about their enhanced learning will be severely restricted.

Idea 1.21
Connective ping-pong!

Holding a ping-pong ball in your hand, make a statement related to your subject and finish that statement with a connective (for example, 'however', 'on the other

(Continued)

(Continued)

hand') and throw the ball to a learner. The learner who catches the ball must continue with another related statement that ends with a connective before throwing the ball to another student, and so on.

 Idea 1.22

Film clips

It pays dividends if you invest the time to collect a range of film clips that relate to your subject area. This is a wonderful way of launching a new subject, theme or concept. Make sure it's dramatic and maintain interest by stopping the clip within a minute of running it to fire questions at named learners. Frame the questions in ways that highlight what learners need to be looking for when watching the clip.

Questions for professional development

1. Do you keep any sort of professional journal? Many trainee teachers do this when learning to become teachers and then give this up once qualified. Journals provide valuable opportunities to reflect on new resources and teaching strategies.
2. Are you a member of a teaching association? Find out which is associated with your subject and join as soon as you can. You will quickly get to know other enthusiastic teachers of your subject, access their resources and gain from their experience of teaching.
3. How quickly can you become a subject examiner? You will be surprised how soon you can do this after qualification, so contact your examination board. Benefits include access to excellent resources, examination-skills training and contact with the people who actually write the examinations your learners will sit.
4. What budget is available from your institution for training? The sooner you can find this out, the greater the opportunity for you to attend outside subject-based training and network with other enthusiastic teachers of your subject.

Checklist: building your toolbox

- Never use the same activities over and over again. Devise a checklist of activities you use and want to use, and aim to introduce a new one every week.
- Make sure that you use a range of resources (even textbooks can vary enormously in the sorts of activities they offer to learners).
- When creating handouts, make sure that you fully utilize your ICT abilities, for example, borders, boxes, speech bubbles can make a huge difference to the ways in which learners respond to handouts and worksheets.
- Try, whenever possible, to use different coloured paper for handouts. Visually this can make a difference to how resources appear on tables and can provide quick information to teachers about which task learners are working on.
- Make sure you have a watch or visible clock in the classroom. Good timing/pace are essential requirements for motivating teenagers. Keep lessons moving and never stay on one activity for too long.
- Do not underestimate the power of your own voice. Shouting is never a good idea but your voice needs to convey authority, enthusiasm, energy and expectation. Audio-record your lesson, focusing on pitch, speed of instruction and tone. Listen to the quality and clarity of your instructions and note any improvements you need to make.
- Teacher mobility around the classroom is essential, so experiment with seating/tables etc and make sure that you can move around easily. This ease of movement will subtlely convey to learners your authority and confidence.

Chapter links

The ideas in this chapter relate closely with those also explored in Chapters 2, 4, 5, 6, 8 and 12.

Further reading

Galton, M., Steward, S., Hargreaves, L., Page C. and Pell, A. (2009) *Motivating Your Secondary Class*. London: Sage.
Although this book is targeting secondary school teachers it contains some fabulous ideas that are transferable to older learners.

Kidd, W., Czerniawski, G. (2010) *Successful Teaching 14–19: Theory, Practice and Reflection*. London: Sage.
This book provides the policy background and theoretical ideas that inform many of our teaching and learning ideas.

CHAPTER 2

FIRST ENCOUNTERS

Chapter overview

The aims of the chapter are to:

1. Provide ideas that enhance the teaching and learning space.
2. Suggest a range of strategies to establish a purposeful working atmosphere and excellent group dynamics.
3. Suggest how the classroom can be used to model organizational skills.
4. Suggest ways in which your learners can co-construct their learning environment.

Problem-solving

We hope that many of you reading this book, whether qualified teachers or teachers in training, have the luxury of your own classrooms or 'base-rooms'. The opportunity to create a classroom atmosphere that is uniquely yours, reflecting your character, aesthetics, interests, passions, knowledge and expectations is to be cherished. But it is also an environment that is shared with your learners, that is, an environment where they have a say in its composition and organization. Get this right and you create the opportunity for learners to step into your own private world and journey with you along a road littered with the golden nuggets of your chosen subject domain. Having your own classroom also means that you can display what you want, when you want and provide an organized methodical learning environment where you and your learners know exactly what to get and where it is located. Such a learning environment can be an invaluable tool in your motivational repertoire, particularly if you can involve your own students in its design, layout and maintenance. However, the reality for most of you reading these pages is that you are probably rushing around from one classroom to the next, carrying a pile of books, a lap-top and a stack of resources, with little time to move furniture, adjust lighting, control heating, replace posters, and so on. However, you will undoubtedly have experienced different sensations on walking into those classrooms that have been lovingly and painstakingly created with a view to maximizing the learning that takes place in those arenas of learning. We hope that this chapter will go some way to helping you create those sorts of environments wherever, and whenever, possible. But be careful – this chapter comes with a health warning! The classroom can be your greatest ally or greatest foe – treat it with respect!

Context

Some of you reading this chapter will be working in buildings dating back to the nineteenth century, while others will be working in spanking new buildings with 'atriums', glass walls and wide open spaces. Laptops, personal computers (PCs) and all sorts of e-learning technology can be turned on and tuned in, however, in some cases learners still seem to be turned off by education (England has one of the lowest staying-on rates in Europe for post-16 learners). Despite the phenomenal growth of teaching resources in recent years and the existence of the best generation of teachers to date, it constantly surprises us how little attention many teachers give to the atmosphere in which learning takes place. Whether you are an experienced or novice teacher, we are sure you have probably, at some stage in your career, encountered resistance by some staff to rearranging the classroom, and we explore this issue more fully in Chapter 6.

This chapter places huge emphasis on what can be done in the classroom to make it a more humane environment, where teenagers will feel energized, motivated and enthused when walking into the learning space you create for them. We hope you will have the confidence to experiment with some of the ideas we offer in this chapter. But creating a learning atmosphere is not just contingent on the bricks, mortar, pot plants and ambience you immerse yourself in. Research, more recently, has focused on the impact of classroom environment on student's motivation (Duncan and McKeachie, 2005; Lee et al., 2009). Hanrahan (1998), for example, found that even though students in an Australian school viewed the classroom environment positively in terms of both intrinsic and extrinsic motivation (see Chapter 1), they felt constrained by too much teacher-centred teaching methods. Your learning environment needs to be flexible enough for you to deploy a range of teaching strategies to meet the diverse needs of your learners. This chapter draws on a range of strategies that you can deploy to create a learning atmosphere that will be the envy of your colleagues and a source of motivation for the young learners in your care.

Toolbox

A room with a view

Think back to when you were at primary school. Chances are that you will imagine a rich, colourful and cosy environment with pockets of activities taking place in different areas of the classroom, reading rugs, plants, things to pick up and mould, and so on. Ceilings will be decorated with word chains, flags, posters and so on. There might have even been the odd hamster trundling perpetually on a wheely walk. These were dynamic environments where active learning, movement and an atmosphere of enquiry were sewn into the fabric of every classroom. Contrast this with the often bland, dull and lifeless environments that typify many secondary and further education (FE) classrooms and it is not surprising that many young people find their transition from primary to secondary education confusing, disturbing and alienating. We recognize how difficult it is for many teachers to have their own base-room and if you are lucky enough to be in this position then you should do everything you can to draw on the excellent practice found in primary school learning environments. If, as is more likely, you move from one classroom to the next, speak to your colleagues and see what you can do to make classrooms places where the learning experience is fun, exploratory, safe, nurturing, cosy, inspiring and motivating.

 Idea 2.1

First impressions

It is easy after a few sessions' teaching in a particular classroom to ignore tatty notice boards, the odd broken chair, the obsolete projector and so on. But for new learners entering your classroom for the very first time many will associate this jaded, tatty environment with the teacher or teachers working in it. Imagine walking into your classroom for the first time and take a detailed look at the room you are about to teach in. Treat it as if it were the sitting room of a flat/house you were considering renting. How would you like it to look and what would annoy you intensely if it was to be a feature of that room? Discard anything that is not functional (for example, obsolete or broken equipment, furniture and so on). Take down (make sure this is acceptable to colleagues) any old displays, posters, notices and so on that have no relevance for your own subject area. Carefully consider how many chairs and tables are actually needed and discard anything that clutters your learning environment. Contact technicians to double check all wiring and so on and tidy up and hide loose cables. Treat the room now as a clean slate and start to create your own ideal learning environment.

 ## Idea 2.2

Remember that primary classroom environment

After following the advice in Idea 2.1, you are now in a position to have some fun transforming the classroom into a learning environment that encourages learners to come into your class regardless of the need to learn your particular subject. What artefacts can you get hold of for your subject area that can be displayed around the room? What 'wow' factor can you create as learners come into your classroom? If you belong to a subject association there will probably be a range of posters, pictures and so on that you can get to decorate walls and ceilings. You can design (better still, get learners to design) time lines that can be placed around the room with significant dates related to your subject area. Key concepts/theories/names can be printed, laminated and displayed around the room (to be used when you teach for short memory games). Magazines are a rich source of visual material that can be artistically displayed. Museums, exhibitions and bookshops are fabulous resources in which to find your classroom displays.

 ## Idea 2.3

Home from home

If you were to make a comparison between classrooms in most primary, secondary and FE institutions, we wonder which you would say bear more resemblance to your own sitting room? It seems strange that while most people happily (and successfully)

(Continued)

(Continued)

study at home surrounded by music, books, plants, carpets, animals, pictures, space to walk around when needed, and so on, the classrooms they find themselves in after primary education bear little or no resemblance to these successful learning environments. What can you do to make your classroom a more homely, stress-free environment? Plants are a must! Many, varied and regularly watered (get students to do this on a rota if necessary). We also encourage the use of music at key moments (for example, as pupils enter the class) in your lessons. Bright, warm colours combined with ventilated rooms are essential 'tools' in successful learning environments. Pictures/posters do not just have to be subject related but can add to the overall ambience of the room. We look at ideal classroom furniture layouts in Chapter 6, but think about the furniture layout of the room and how best it suits a variety of different activities, and whether or not learners and you can move easily around the classroom.

 Reflection point

Remember that some of your learners will not necessarily come from domestic environments where formal learning has taken place or, in some cases, is particularly highly valued. This means that while some students will have very clear ideas about the sort of learning environment they would like to create (or re-create) at home, others will have little or no idea (or motivation) to do this once they leave your classroom. This places you in a powerful position to 'model' learning and studying practices that can then be exported into the home by those students who may not have other suitable role models.

 Idea 2.4

Modelling study environments

Never underestimate the influence you can have on learners – particularly when we talk about modelling certain study practices. Again, we turn to the primary classroom for inspiration here. Make sure that everything has a place in your classroom. Book shelves need to be labelled and books neatly categorized and replaced after use. Boxes of all shapes and sizes can be bought to store pencils, rubbers, files, and so on, all of which can be colour coded (you can create a poster with a colour code if necessary). Contact the administration person in your school/college and ask him or her to have a look at the education stationer's catalogue. You will be amazed at what exists to help you create that 'model' learning environment.

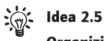 **Idea 2.5**

Organizing student folders

Part of the learning environment you create will comprise the work that students bring to your classrooms. Following on from Idea 2.4 above, many learners do not necessarily come 'armed' with the sorts of organizational skills required to study as they get older. Folder checks can be an invaluable way of modelling this and we strongly advise regular structured checks of their folders and portfolios. Ideally keep a past folder available so that students can see how best this is done (for example, plastic wallets that are labelled, dividers). All your learners should feel that this is an essential part of their learning experience with you.

Best practice – give students ownership of their own learning environment

When creating classrooms for new learners, practitioners have found it useful to consider the following:

- If appropriate and you have access to finances take some students to the local supermarket and get them to choose pot plants to decorate their classroom. Different learners can then be nominated to look after the plants on a monthly basis.
- Get students to bring in their own (appropriate) posters, pictures, artefacts to be displayed around the classroom.
- Nominate different students to choose 'music for the week' that will be played as students come into your classroom.
- If classrooms are to be painted over the holiday period get students to choose the colour scheme (many schools now do this through 'Student Voice' initiatives).
- As a classroom management strategy keep back those students who have not been working in the way you feel suitable – and get them to tidy the classroom, move furniture back, and so on.

Establishing a purposeful atmosphere when taking over a new class

Ensure, wherever and whenever possible, you are in the classroom before your students. Quickly and efficiently lay out your resources, paperwork, attendance records, and so on so that no time is wasted or lost during that all-important arrival of the class. Scan the room quickly as you move around, and tidy any chairs and tables. First impressions count, and the sight of you standing at the door to a clean and orderly classroom will subconsciously affect how students perceive you and their learning environment. Remember that you can be friendly with students but your job is not to be their 'friend'. This means that you must juggle the difficult job of creating mutual respect between teacher and learner while providing clear boundaries, not just between you and your learners but also between each activity. This requires meticulous planning, resourcing and orchestration of a range of activities designed to meet the needs of your learners.

 Reflection point

Do you know your school/college behaviour management escalation policy? This is really important as, while you may posses imaginative and creative ideas about how to establish rules and so on, you must make sure that these are in line with your institution's codes of conduct/behaviour. For example is it acceptable in your institution to send somebody out of the classroom or give them a detention? Students need to know the 'ladder of escalation', that is, understand what stage they might be at and where they could possibly go next.

 Idea 2.6

Classroom behaviour plan

While we certainly argue that classrooms should be warm, fun environments full of enquiry and engaging activities, boundaries are essential for efficient activities, particularly when classroom numbers can be large. When taking over a class, establish a code of behaviour from the outset. One way of doing this is the use of students to draft (this can be done in groups) their top ten 'dos and don'ts' in the classroom. For younger learners this could be done by getting them to think of their class as a country, with a flag and so on and getting them to think up 'ten rules of the realm'. Adhering to these is made all the more powerful when students know that they have generated their own code.

 Idea 2.7

Be consistent!

While most learners will be very willing to do what you wish them to do in their first lesson with you they will also be watching intensely to see what sort of teacher you are, and whether or not you have the highest expectations of them. Part of their apprenticeship of observation will be to see if you actually follow through on what you say you will do. You must be relentless in this. If you say that you wish to talk to a student about something, ensure that you do (even if this means using your break to find out where they are in the building at any given time). Once students see that you are relentless and follow up any issue (for example, lack of homework, lateness, inappropriate behaviour and so on) they will think twice before repeating their actions. Other learners will quickly respect you for your professional actions (even if they don't necessarily always like the outcome).

 Idea 2.8

Own your classroom

Getting to that classroom very early allows you, the teacher, to move furniture, adjust blinds, turn on equipment and so on. But it does so much more than that. It fills you with a sense of 'ownership' over the classroom space and learners very quickly (albeit subconsciously) pick up on this and the confidence this conveys. Stand at the door and confidently greet students, directing them to where you wish them to sit. Refer to key named students and get them to give things out, place things on, move to and so on – this is a confidence marker and will help in the pace and delivery of the early stages of any lesson. At every stage of the lesson confidently move around the classroom and make sure learners see you watching them. Be quick to smile and praise activities in the early part of the lesson but also be quick to pick up on inappropriate behaviour. This will 'set the scene' for your high expectations of the rest of the lesson. Pre-empt non-desirable behaviour by moving to those areas of the classroom you feel such behaviour may initiate.

Best practice – back to basics

When creating a learning environment in your classroom, learners need to feel that you are confident and in control but they also need to feel respected and trusted by you and their classroom colleagues. They need to feel that you know their strengths and weaknesses and how you you might be able to improve their ability to learn and succeed in their subject. Consider the following suggestions.

- Organize your classroom neatly and methodically to minimize confusion and stress. All learners need to be able to find books and materials at all times.

(Continued)

(Continued)

- Inject trust into all relationships you form with students. Allocate roles to them that convey this trust, for example, ask individuals to be student representatives; invite them to certain staff meetings.
- Use your body, voice and facial expressions to inject pace and dynamics into your lessons. Keep a constant check on all learners and let them see that you are doing this. If attention levels flag, adjust your lesson plan accordingly and be prepared to inject a new activity to compensate.
- Your energy levels will be replicated by theirs, so keep mobile and make sure your voice is animated and enthusiastic, particularly when issuing instructions for the next task.
- Greet students at the door warmly and make sure that you put 'yesterday behind you' in the case of any student that has been reprimanded by you. Notice any students with new bags, items of clothing, and so on, and be prepared to comment favourably, that is, show an interest in them as they enter so that they get to see your interest in them as people and not just students.

Establishing group dynamics

We said at the start of this chapter that bricks and mortar alone, however funky and however imaginatively put together, cannot by themselves ensure an ideal learning environment. You also need the social cement that will be the foundations for the interactive and supportive learning that is so crucial to motivating young learners. When taking over new classes it is important to break down barriers as quickly as possible so that you can create the right sort of classroom dynamics for learning to take place. It is also important for your learners to see you confidently manipulating the classroom in imaginative and creative ways. The following activities are suggestions to create the rapport, empathy and good humour required when taking over classes for the first time and when students do not yet know each other.

 Idea 2.9

Game for a name

This activity is noisy and will require space made in the centre of your classroom for learners to move around. Arrange seating in one large circle facing inwards. Going first anti-clockwise and then clockwise, ask each person to call out their name so that all have heard a name twice. Now ask one volunteer to run to the chair of somebody else while calling out their name. That person must, in turn, vacate their chair, run to another person and call their name, and so on. This highly energetic activity is designed to quickly break down barriers.

Idea 2.10

A square deal

This task works best when students are sat in groups of three to four. Give to each member of your class a sheet of paper that is made up of one large square with four smaller ones in it. Instruct the class to write down four bits of information about themselves, three of which must be lies, and the fourth of which must be true. Each group must tease out from each member which fact is true.

Idea 2.11

The survival game

This classic activity is a great way of generating classroom discussion and debate. It is particularly useful when teasing out similarities and differences in cultures, ideologies and genders but works well purely as a method of establishing and teaching about group dynamics. Get your new class to sit in groups of four or five learners. Inform them that they are flying as passengers on a jumbo jet over the Pacific. By chance a nuclear war takes place during their flight, disrupting the aircraft's instruments and forcing the captain to ditch close to a small island. Shortly before landing the captain learns via the radio that they are about to become the last remaining survivors on the planet. The job of each group is to decide what sort of society they can create on the island. Questions that might help the groups could be: what needs to be arranged immediately? How will tasks be arranged? How will decisions be made? How will children be looked after? How will family life be sorted? What happens to rule breakers? Stand back and watch as your learners grapple with some fundamental philosophical and sociological debates.

 Reflection point

Are you orchestrator or conductor? We referred earlier to the job of teacher as an 'orchestrator', that is, the one that does not play but arranges, organizes and

(Continued)

(Continued)

coordinates the music that is played. But your job in these activities goes beyond orchestration and includes conducting what can be very complex individual and group interactions. It is essential that in these processes you monitor everything and guard against any inappropriate interactions between students. Your job is to seamlessly move students from one transition point to the next so that they gain the maximum enjoyment and learning in the short space of time that you have with them. The success of both conductor and orchestrator roles will hinge on the meticulous lesson planning you put in place prior to any lesson you teach.

 Idea 2.12

Architect

While this activity will require a range of resources before you start the lesson and a significant space after the lesson to display the work your students produce, this activity is a fabulous way of building teamwork and cooperative skills. Split the class into groups of four or five pupils. Provide each group with a range of resources that will enable them to construct a building (for example, school, hospital, leisure centre). Give them basic stationery resources (sticky tape, straws, card, toilet roll tubes, cardboard, and so on). Even better – ask them to bring in any resources they can do from home (we have seen this done with pupils in a school being asked to bring in the contents of their kitchen rubbish). Give them 60–90 minutes, telling them that their work will be displayed somewhere prominent in the institution.

 Idea 2.13

Back to back

This simple paired task will help foster cooperation between individual students and is really easy to facilitate. Ask learners to sit back to back. One person has a picture or an image or any information you feel suitable. They must describe it to the other who simultaneously draws what they hear until they can guess what the item might be.

 Idea 2.14

Triangular interviews

This is an easy way to introduce a range of essential skills to a class you are taking over and supplying you with important information about their hobbies, likes, dislikes and so on. Tables are not necessary for this activity and, if possible, move tables to the sides of the classroom. Seat learners in groups of three numbering each student '1', '2' and '3'. Get the 1s to interview the 2s while the 3s take notes. These interviews are short biographical details to be fed back to the class by way of introduction. Keep interviews short (maximum 3 minutes) and then ask the scribes to feedback to the whole class. Repeat, changing the roles until all learners have been interviewed.

 Idea 2.15

My other half

This involves a little preparation and space in the classroom (so move tables and chairs to the sides) but the movement, laughter and energy this creates is worth the effort when establishing group dynamics. Divide the class into two halves, with one half given questions and the other given answers to those questions. Learners must go around the room trying to find out who their partner is.

Questions for professional development

1. When you observe other teachers in different classrooms, to what extent do you take on board the classroom environment in which they teach? In what ways do you think the teacher considers that environment is a significant factor in the teaching and learning that takes place?
2. What limitations do you have in creating your own ideal learning environment? Write these down and discuss them with your mentors/line managers and so on.
3. What is there outside the classroom (for example, galleries, museums, woods, people) that you can incorporate within your teaching and learning? Devise a list of organizations you can contact and ask to donate artefacts and so on that you can use to liven up your classroom.
4. In what ways can you involve food in the teaching of your subject? Food, the ultimate cross-curricular resource, can be a fantastic source of fun, nutrition, curiosity and, above all, knowledge. Inject some fun by asking students to bring in food related to their culture, subject or locality. Devise a list of activities that involve their contributions to the teaching of your subject area.

Checklist: building your toolbox

- Always consider the temperature and air circulation in any room you teach. Check thermostats, open windows and doors when necessary, turn off computers when not needed and use fans in the summer. The more plants you have the better.

- Hydration and nutrition are crucial to the learning process. Make sure your learners have access to water and encourage them to eat healthily (particularly in the build-up to any formal examination).
- Stress does not complement learning. Use music during your lessons (for example, as students arrive, or when they are involved in discussions) to create a calm learning environment. Ensure students know what to do and when to avoid chaotic transitions. Introduce students to any assessment criteria well in advance of any formal examination, to reduce last-minute panic.
- The best classroom environments are those where students feel intellectually challenged but where that challenge is 'laddered', that is learners believe they can make it to the next step. Combine fun activities with an air of competition (between individuals and groups) to help create that environment.
- Motivation can be considerably increased if learners have a say in their learning and the environment in which they learn. Involve your learners in the evaluation of your lessons and ask them what activities work best for them. Use their feedback to inform the planning and the resourcing of your lessons.
- Happy learners will learn far more effectively than unhappy ones. Use praise regularly but diligently. Inject fun activities at key moments in your lesson to maintain energy levels and the buzz of enthusiasm. Celebrate learners' work with the occasional prize and display any exemplary homework/classwork.
- The experience of being inside the classroom environment can be drastically improved by being outside it. Research museums, walks, galleries, plays, films, and so on that will bring to life your own subject.
- Mutual respect, justice and support are essential ingredients in any classroom. Make sure you earn respect rather than expect it from your learners. Ensure that you possess the highest expectations of your own professional practice as well as their learning.

Chapter links

The ideas in this chapter relate closely with those also explored in Chapters 1, 4, 5 and 8.

Further reading

Gilbert, I. (2002) *Essential Motivation in the Classroom*. London: RoutledgeFalmer.
An accessible small text providing a comprehensive overview of motivational theory.

Kidd, W. and Czerniawski, G. (2010) *Successful Teaching 14–19: Theory, Practice and Reflection*. London: Sage.
In this, our other book, we consider more fully the theoretical and practical implications of first encounters.

Marland, M. (1993) *The Craft of the Classroom*. London: Heinemann.
An invaluable text for those new to teaching.

CHAPTER 3

ASSESSMENT STRATEGIES FOR MOTIVATING LEARNERS

Chapter overview

The aims of the chapter are to:

1. Introduce the reader to formative, summative and ipsative assessment strategies.
2. Highlight the connection between assessment and motivation.
3. Offer guidance on the conditions in which assessment should be carried out.
4. Suggest a range of ideas that provide invaluable feedback on teaching and learning.

Problem-solving

The word 'assessment' for many potential teachers conjures up images of examinations, essays and a stack of exercise books to mark. In fact assessment, when correctly and skilfully carried out, can motivate and inspire learners to perform beyond their own expectations in all formal learning scenarios. So what do we mean by 'assessment'? When planning lessons it helps to think of four broad strategies. First, *initial* or *diagnostic* assessment refers to tasks that occur at the start of any course/unit/module designed to measure if the course the learner is on is best suited to the learner. Typically it looks at the sorts of support a student might require (for example, literacy, numerary). Second, *summative* assessment refers to 'snapshots' taken at any one time, of a learner's progress (for example, public examinations, end of term tests). While this provides vital information for both learner and teacher, most summative assessments offer little or no information to inform the future progress of the learner. Third, *formative* assessment is any type of assessment that informs that future progress. It is often ongoing and can be informally carried out (for example, a corridor chat with a student to offer advice on the next assignment) or formally carried out (for example, written feedback with targets at the end of an essay/report). Finally *ipsative* assessment refers to the process of learner self-assessment, that is, the learner identifies his or her own progress and identifies his or her own needs. It is also a form of assessment that recognizes the progress made by the individual regardless of any external benchmarks. All four strategies come in a variety of shapes and sizes to be carried out informally and formally, and these underpin the ideas contained within this chapter.

Context

Assessment, as a topic of research, is not new and some (not all) of the tools and strategies we introduce you to in this chapter are typical of the sorts of strategies that excellent teachers have been doing for generations. However, over the past decade a renewed focus on different ways of assessing has emerged since the work of Black and Wiliam's (1998) *Inside the Black Box* and the Assessment Reform Group (2002). Their conclusions are both a source of inspiration and caution to the teaching profession. Black and Wiliam argue that while regular formative assessment is extremely effective in raising academic standards, assessment practices in general have often been little understood by the teaching profession. Evidence from the Assessment Reform Group has shown that how assessment of learning is reported back to the learner (feedback) affects their motivation to learn. This body of work has led to renewed attention on the adoption of so-called 'medal and mission' assessment strategies. The 'medal' relates to any positive aspects of the work being assessed and the 'mission' draws the learner's attention to targets for future learning. This 'formative' emphasis on the nature and purpose of assessment prioritizes 'feedforward' over and above 'feedback', suggesting that better school/college results will follow from better learning and by developing and maintaining pupils' motivation to learn, rather than an overemphasis on the often demotivating effects of summative testing.

Toolbox

Between two worlds

Teachers are often caught between two conflicting assessment models – those that are norm referenced and those that are criterion referenced. The former refers to marks that are allocated on a 'quota' against a notional 'normal' distribution of learners taking the assessment task (for example, the A grades that vary each year in public examinations such as GCSEs and A levels). In this case the learning cohort is banded together and measured against each other – hence the term 'norm'. The latter refers to those learners judged against skills or competencies outlined at the start of the course, success being defined by those students that achieve those skills or competencies. Both models have the capacity to demotivate learners who might feel that they are not 'performing' to the level expected. Increasingly, criterion-based assessment is driving public examinations, causing many teachers to worry about those learners (for example, those whose first language might not be English) who might see themselves as 'failing' despite the remarkable improvements they might be making on their courses. It is therefore essential that teachers include other forms of assessment if they are to continue to motivate teenage learners, even when those learners might be seen to be failing within national or local parameters.

Ipsative assessment and SPACE

Ipsative assessment is any form of assessment that highlights the development (or 'distance travelled') that an individual learner makes regardless of external benchmarks. At its best it exemplifies the reflective ability of the learner to assess their own work and initiate targets for improvement. Successful ipsative assessment strategies should be:

- **S**ensitive to the learning context and individual learner.
- **P**romoting self-worth, motivation and subject development.
- **A**daptable, flexible and responsive to changing contexts.
- **C**ollaborative and owned by learners.
- **E**valuative and act as a bridge between one learning activity and the next.

Idea 3.1
Definitely maybe

This activity combines peer assessment, self-assessment and teacher assessment in a powerful way to focus on the reflective skills needed to be lifelong learners. In groups of three or four, learners pass their work (ideally at an interim stage, rather than the end product) to the rest of the group in turn. When their work returns to them it will have a Post-it note from each group member with two things they liked and one area for improvement (against the assessment criteria). Sticking the Post-its on a separate sheet, the learner writes next to each whether they agree with the suggestions or not, justifying their decision each time. The teacher then comments where necessary on the suggestions and the learner's decision to accept or reject each suggestion, before the learner uses the process to inform the next draft of their work.

Idea 3.2
Questioning strategies

As an assessment strategy the use of questioning can measure not only the progress of your learners but your own teaching strategies. Questioning techniques vary. Socratic questioning attempts to draw out answers from learners, for example; 'What do you mean by that?' or 'Can you explain that?' Rolling questions are those that build knowledge by moving from one learner to the next with each learner response leading to another question. 'Traffic-directing' is a strategy whereby learners ask questions of each other and the teacher facilitates the direction and flow of questions as and when necessary. Alternatively, move learners through the processes of recall, definition, application, synthesis and evaluation (Bloom, 1956b). Do this by creating questions that move through each of these processes, firing questions from one learner to the next. When combined with teacher mobility in the classroom, questioning acts as a significant classroom management tool. See Chapter 11 for more discussion of questioning.

Idea 3.3
Questioning strategy with the 5Ws

This task is useful for encouraging evaluation skills. Choose an evocative or controversial photograph related to your subject area. Ask learners what they think is going on by focusing on the five Ws (What? Where? When? Why? Who? – you can always add an 'H' for 'How?). Target questions at named students in your classes scattering the questions across the classroom (that is, front, back and sides). This idea can be adapted to any artefact you decide to bring into the classroom by asking learners to devise five questions to ask that, when answered, will explain what the object is.

Idea 3.4

Sift and sort

This commonly used idea is great for assessing knowledge of key terms and concepts. Print off, laminate and guillotine 20 key terms with their associated definitions and place in envelopes on the desks. Learners can match up on their own or in pairs. Have fun by injecting competition for the first pair that get the correct order.

Idea 3.5

Kinaesthetic true/false

Display a contentious statement on the board and ask learners to move to one end of the class if they feel the statement is true and to the opposite end if they believe the statement is false. Once in position, fire questions at the learners to justify their position in the line.

Best practice – the Assessment Reform Group (2002)

The Assessment Reform Group (2002) has suggested some key principles to follow when using assessment and testing to motivate learning. These include:

- Creating a learning environment where learners can learn collaboratively.
- Allowing for, and accommodating as much learner choice as possible.
- Encouraging learners to take responsibility for assessment of their learning.
- Illustrating the purpose of learning to all learners and showing where this fits in within the wider context of the subject being studied.
- Connecting learning, wherever possible, to previous and future learning.
- Framing feedback ('feedforward') in such a way that learners are clear what to do next and why.

Reflection point

Inspired by the work of Black and Wiliam (1998) many teachers, when working with younger teenagers, adopt the use of a 'traffic light' approach to learner self-assessment and feedback. Learners grade work or lessons 'RED' for difficult, 'AMBER' for moderately OK and 'GREEN' for easy. This unconfrontational and unimposing method of assessment is one incorporating learner voice as part of your emerging picture of learners. It is a method that can be adopted and combined with kinaesthetic learning strategies (for example, the allocation of group-based tasks geographically placed in the classroom, where learners choose to go to the area of the class and work at the prescribed level).

 Idea 3.6

Humpty Dumpty

Scaffolding activities, that is ensuring that learners move easily from one stage of a task to the next, is essential to avoid the demotivation that can occur as a result of 'failing' a task – particularly significant when preparing learners for public examinations. Combine this with peer-supported activities and learners can quickly develop the sorts of examination skills required to achieve success. Cut up a model answer/ exemplar essay (best to laminate this so you can use it again and again) and place it in an envelope. Distribute this to pairs of learners asking them to work together to reconstruct the paragraphs in the order in which the essay was written. Distribute mark schemes to each pair and get them to 'mark' the essay justifying why they award the mark they do. You can offer a mini-prize for the pair that give the correct mark. Can you say more about how and why this works? Why is it a good idea?

 Idea 3.7

Chief examiner for a day

The following activity is excellent for getting students to understand what examiners are looking for. The activity, in reality, recreates the training that many examiners get shortly before they mark public examinations. Obtain from examination boards exemplar passed past papers with known marks and the accompanying mark scheme (you can always create your own if you prefer). Make sure you have three papers (try to photocopy these in three different colours) that represent high, medium and low mark bands. Each learner gets a set of the three exemplars and the mark scheme. Working on their own or in pairs learners have to decide what mark they are going to award. Their job is to get as close to the correct marks you have already decided.

 Reflection point

Concept mapping/brainstorming is a strategy for organizing information encouraging learners to integrate multiple sources of information, including visual images, emotional responses and written words. Integrating these into a symbolic system helps learners organize large quantities of information while developing a range of thinking skills associated with knowledge, understanding, interpretation, application and evaluation of the topic being investigated. These diagrams/drawings can be used to generate, visualize, structure and classify ideas, and as an aid to studying and organizing information, solving problems, making decisions, and writing.

 Idea 3.8

Collective concept mapping/brainstorming

Quite often learners are unsure what brainstorming/concept mapping actually is. Your role is to model this particular activity for them. This works best if you can access the many free mind-mapping programmes available to download from the Internet. Ask learners for key ideas from the last lesson/current module, ensuring that their books are closed. Collate a collective mindmap on your smartboard. This activity can be extended into homework by asking learners to create their own concept map based on the key words generated in class.

For examples of mindmaps go to http://www.thinkbuzan.com/uk/support/tutorials

Best practice – SMART

Remember that all instructions and feedback should be:

- Specific, that is, refer exactly to what students should do rather than issuing instructions or praise that is generalized and vague.
- Measurable, that is, any activity should have an outcome that the teacher can identify (for example, one speech, one photograph, one whole paragraph of writing).

(Continued)

(Continued)

- Achievable, that is, the task should challenge the learner but not be something they cannot achieve. It can be incredibly demotivating to set out on a piece of work and realize you cannot achieve its outcome.
- Realistic, that is, it must be something the learner can do (for example, if a learner does not posses a television it will be impossible for them to do an analysis of television advertisements).
- Timed, that is, assessment tasks need to be set within a time limit (for example, 'you have 10 minutes to . . .' or 'this homework must be handed in by 2.00 p.m. on Friday').

 Idea 3.9

The domino effect

This is another activity that checks knowledge and understanding of key concepts. Create a set of dominoes on paper or card (for example, with a key word/concept on half of an A4 sheet and with a definition on the other half). This can be done manually by you or you can download software that enables this to be done quickly. Give each group of four learners a pack of the dominoes (make sure that you never have the correct definition and key word on the same card). The winning group is the one that correctly lines up the dominoes.

Who are we trying to assess?

Teachers often work in distinct 'communities of practice' (Wenger, 1998) with particular understandings about what 'works best' in different subjects (for example, teachers of mathematics may have very different ideas about the sorts of assessment strategies they may wish to adopt, compared with history teachers). This next section introduces you to ideas on how to assess your own learners that will challenge, stretch and motivate teenagers. While we fully recognize that many of you reading this book will be focused on getting students ready for public examinations, think too about how assessment can inspire, motivate and inform the future progress of not only your learners, but you – the teacher.

 Reflection point

The following list consists of a range of assessment tools most commonly in use: examinations (actual and 'mock'); essays; stimulus response questions; witness statements and testimonials; posters; practicals; performance; wiki chat; mobile phone imagery; blog contributions; presentations; role plays; case study evalua-tions; diaries/journals; vivas; exhibitions; podcasts; videos. Consider how each of these common assessment tools could be adapted to meet formative, summative and ipsative purposes.

Idea 3.10
House of cards

This memory-based activity is fun and great for reinforcing concepts. Use a nor-mal pack of playing cards and deal one out to each member of the class. Ask them to remember or write down their card giving the cards back to you. Use only the cards you have given out. Read out a card and whoever 'is' that card has to recall one fact/concept from your lesson. Read out the next card and that person has to remember a new fact and the previous one mentioned and so on.

Idea 3.11
In my head

Using empathy can be a powerful way for learners to reflect and evaluate what it might have been like to be in a particular context (for example, political pro-tests, assassinations). Choose an emotive picture (for example, historical draw-ings of people watching public executions) and project this onto your smartboard/whiteboard. Ask learners to draw their own face on a Post-it note and stick this onto the face of somebody in the picture. Once they return to their tables, get them to write down what that person might be thinking and then ask them to stick this under the picture of their own faces. Learners can then go up in groups and look at the contributions from the class.

Idea 3.12
Jigsaw memory

This is another task that boosts the confidence of learners to memorize and engage with new material. Take any article and split this into sections; then jigsaw (see Chapter 4) it, that is, split the class into three or six groups and give each group a section to read – explaining to them that they must memorize the contents (not word for word but key facts/information). Make sure this is carried out in strict

(Continued)

(Continued)

silence and do not allow them to take notes during this activity. Ignore the protestations (you can do this lightheartedly but explain to them that you have great faith in their ability to memorize large bits of information). Collect all the material in and then allow each group to help each other to remember what was in the text and to write down all they can remember. Now split the groups up (this can be done by numbering them to re-form new groups). You will now have new groups formed with representatives for each part of the article. Get everybody to share information (you can produce a pro forma with boxes to aid this) before sending them back to their home groups to tease out key concepts, theories, people, and so on.

Idea 3.13

Bubble and squeak

This idea is useful to deploy when learners come to the end of a particular module, unit, and so on. Give learners two pieces of paper and ask them to write their strongest topic on one piece and weakest topic on another. Ask learners to move around the room until they find people whose strengths complement their own weaknesses and allow them to peer teach each other.

Idea 3.14

Box and cox

This activity is a simple and unthreatening way of assessing to what extent learners have understood your teaching. At the end of any lesson, ask students to write down two questions that relate to something they do not understand. Make sure these are anonymous and ask them to put these into a box prepared by you. You can quickly go through any questions and clarify issues to the class that they may not have understood.

 Reflection point

When evaluating different assessment strategies, reflect on the following criteria when assessing how effective they are:

1. Is it valid, that is, does it assess what it is supposed to?
2. Is it reliable, that is, can the assessment and its judgement be repeated by another teacher or with another group under the same conditions with similar results?

3. It is adequate/sufficient, that is, is the data sufficient to tell you what you need to know about the group, the learner and your teaching strategies?
4. Is it fair, that is, can all students engage with the tasks and is support available to those that cannot?
5. Is it appropriate, that is, does it develop skills needed for the particular programme of study?
6. Is it authentic, that is, is the work being assessed the work of the student submitting it?
7. Is it transparent, that is, do all those being assessed understand what they are being asked to do and why?

 Idea 3.15

Pass the parcel

This is a fun activity and is useful for assessing the knowledge of learners at the start of a new unit/topic/module. While playing music, pass around a box filled with statements about the topic you will be studying in the lesson. When the music stops, the student with the box must pick out a statement, read it and decide whether it is true or false.

 Idea 3.16

Oops – spot the mistake

This is a simple method to check overall understanding of a topic and iron out any misconceptions before moving on to something more complex. Project a small passage onto the board with deliberate mistakes made (for example, spelling mistakes, incorrect definitions matched to terms, dates). Get students in pairs to identify how many mistakes they can spot and what the correct version should look like. This activity can also be done individually by using a handout.

 Idea 3.17

All fingers and thumbs

This activity is a variation of brainstorming and provides opportunities for you to assess to what extent learners have a grasp of the key elements that make up your topic area. It also provides an invaluable (for some) way of revision. Get

(Continued)

(Continued)

learners to draw an outline of their hands onto a piece of A3 paper. Now get them to identify the main building blocks of their subject and allocate them to various parts of the palms of their drawn hands. They can then use the fingers and thumbs to represent master concepts and smaller concepts. We have, on more than one occasion, seen students in examinations holding out their hands and remembering key concepts related to their topics.

Idea 3.18

Question grand prix

This deliberately competitive activity works best in pairs and initially will take some time to prepare, but it is well worth it. Prepare a box with lots of questions (start with the principle that you will require a minimum of 10 questions per student and then you will probably have more than enough). You can always raid past examination questions if necessary. Start with the first question projected onto the board and get students in pairs to answer on paper (short answers in full sentences work best). The moment they have answered this, one member will rush to show it to you – if you are happy with their response reach into the box and pull out the next question. Award a prize to the pair that answer the most questions.

Questions for professional development

1. In what ways are the data compiled about your students used to assess the performance of the teachers who teach in the institution? To what extent do you believe that such data are useful in serving this purpose?
2. In what ways can you build in more ipsative strategies of assessment in your teaching? To what extent is 'distance travelled' more meaningful to you as a teacher than norm- or criterion-based assessment data?
3. To what extent do you carry out your own diagnostic assessments on learners when taking over classes, and to what extent to you rely on information provided by your institution? Are both these elements always in harmony? What sort of diagnostic test could you incorporate as part of your induction of new learners?
4. When working for the first time with learners who have just come from another school/college, to what extent do you look at their records/reports/examination results? Do you know where such records are kept within your own institution? Have you got easy access to these records?

Checklist: building your toolbox

- Ensure that you always carry out a diagnostic assessment when working with new learners.
- Whenever possible make sure you are aware of who taught your students prior to their arrival with you. If they have come from another institution, find out if they experienced any learning difficulties.
- Trust your professional instincts when your own assessment strategies and records highlight discrepancies in records passed on to you by previous colleagues/institutions (for example, many cases of dyslexia are first spotted by vigilant colleagues working in sixth form centres and FE colleges, despite those learners having attended primary and secondary schools and the disability going unnoticed).
- When working with students who are taking public examinations, ensure that you are fully aware of all documentation coming from the examination boards. Mark schemes and model answers are invaluable day-to-day tools for the teacher; however, far fewer teachers use examiners' reports. These wonderful documents will give you insightful information about what exactly examiners are looking for and will highlight trends and common pitfalls made by many students.
- Try to ensure that all your assessment feedback, whether spoken or written, is SMART feedback.
- When considering assessment, try not to confine yourself within your own community of practice. Keep an eye on the sorts of assessments used in other subject areas that learners like, and see which of those ideas you can adopt in your own subject area.

Chapter links

The ideas in this chapter relate closely with those also explored in Chapters 5, 9 and 12.

Further reading

Assessment Reform Group (1999) *Assessment for Learning: Beyond the Black Box*. Cambridge: University of Cambridge School of Education.
Assessment Reform Group (2002) *Testing, Motivation and Learning*. Cambridge: University of Cambridge School of Education.
Black, P. and Wiliam, D. (1998) *Inside the Black Box: Raising Standards through Classroom Assessment*. London: NferNelson.
The above three recommended readings provide an excellent overview of assessment for learning and accompanying strategies.

CHAPTER 4

TEACHING TO ENGAGE

Chapter overview

The aims of the chapter are to:

1. Provide strategies for teachers to easily move learners in classrooms when engaging in group-based active-learning activities.
2. Introduce teaching ideas that reduce the ratio of teacher talk to pupil talk.
3. Consider the importance of classroom environment when motivating teenage learners.
4. Understand the significance of teacher rapport when generating dynamic pupil-led conversation.

Problem-solving

In this chapter, we consider how to fully engage students in their learning by concentrating on the role that movement and classroom-talk can have in raising levels of motivation in teenage learners. Engaged learners do not simply go through the motions of each task they are set, but are immersed in the theories, concepts, debates and evidence that make up their subject. We recognize the difficulties in getting learners to engage in targeted discussions designed to raise achievement while simultaneously avoiding opportunities for low- high-level disruption. The ideas in this chapter are designed to avoid these pitfalls and add to your repertoire of motivational skills. We believe that successful classroom discussion and 'group work' are not activities that can be thrown together on a whim. Teaching to engage requires careful planning and orchestration that often leads to noisy but creative and exciting learning environments. With this in mind the ideas in this chapter are concerned with shifting the balance away from too much teacher talk to focusing on the importance of movement and productive learner discussion in your lessons. As long as the teacher manages and harnesses learner interaction carefully, and consults with colleagues beforehand, a noisy classroom (providing it is the right kind of noise) can motivate and inspire all teenage learners.

Context

There are many reasons why it is important to build movement into any classroom environment. Reiss's theory on intrinsic motivation (2000) states that physical activity is one of many basic desires that directly motivates a person's behaviour. For many children and adults, sitting still for hours does not provide the ideal learning environment to meet their individual learning needs. Bandler and Grinder's (1981) pioneering work on neurolinguistic programming (NLP) argues that our internal sensory representations are constantly being formed and activated. It is therefore the job of the teacher to stimulate each and every one of our five senses for successful teaching to take place. In practice, many schools, colleges and teachers draw on Bandler and Grinder, referring to visual, auditory and kinaesthetic ('VAK') learning styles in relation to NLP when creating resources or planning lessons. Futhermore, keeping teenagers immobile behind desks in crowded classrooms runs counterintuitively to Howard Gardner's (1993) work on multiple intelligences. In contrast to the nineteenth-century conception of intelligence as singular, logical and rational, Gardner argues that we have a variety of 'intelligences', including 'bodily kinaesthetic' intelligence as exemplified by athletes, dancers and other physical performers. Keeping teenagers immobile for long periods of time in crowded classrooms will therefore work against the interests of those learners said to possess higher levels of this particular intelligence. As a rule of thumb, we would therefore argue that good teaching requires movement to be built into your teaching repertoire.

Toolbox

Moving learners around the room

Moving and regrouping learners enables effective differentiation through the strategic grouping of learners based upon characteristics and needs. Moving can also stop learners from feeling tired and bored. Regrouping enables learners to mix and, thus, build a stronger sense of group identity over time. Teachers can place greater emphasis (in both the planning and delivery processes) upon student talk and interaction as a prime vehicle through which learning takes place. The ideas that follow offer strategies to easily move learners around the classroom while keeping them firmly focused on their learning outcomes.

Idea 4.1

Jigsaw

Aronson et al.'s (1978) active learning technique is one of the most common ways of moving teenage learners to ensure they sit with different members during the course of any lesson and engage in productive learner-centred talk. Ensure tables are arranged in groups (called 'home groups') with between three to five people at each table and that there are different texts, pictures, and so on with each home group. Instruct the groups to take notes on the materials they have in front of them. After an appropriate time number each learner in each group ('Group A, remember your numbers: 1, 2, 3, 4'; 'Group B, remember your numbers: 1, 2, 3, 4', and so on). After you have done this, make sure the class can see that you allocate a number to each of the home group tables ('Ladies and gentleman, this table is now table 1, this table is now table 2', and so on). Once all learners are clear about their own numbers and which table they will move to, move them according to their number (all number 1s, move to table 1, all number 2s to table 2' and so on). You have now re-formed groups with completely different members. If necessary you can return learners to their home groups to collate information or work on a new task.

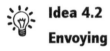

Idea 4.2

Envoying

Form 'home groups' (see Idea 4.1) at the start of the lesson. Learners in these groups will be working on set tasks where information-gathering is crucial. Each home group will be working with different information. Give groups time to summarize and then choose one 'envoy' from each group to go to another group to transfer that group's information as well as picking up new information from the group visited. Send them back to their home group and collate all information gathered.

Idea 4.3

Lollipop sticks

Arrange and clearly number tables in groups before the lesson. Have a collection (enough for each member of your class) of lollipop sticks with a number on (ensure the number corresponds with the amount of grouped tables you have in the class). As each learner comes into your class give them a lollipop stick and ask them to sit at that table. Lollipop sticks with learners' names on can also be used to randomly ask for student contributions, asking questions, and so on.

 Idea 4.4

Circuit training

The classroom is arranged in a series of 'islands', each containing a different activity. You can label each table with a coloured title describing to learners what the nature of the activity is. As they arrive they put their bags and coats to the side, so that they are not an obstacle as they move, and in pairs or threes they sit at a table of their choice (depending on overall class numbers). Each activity must be short (maximum 10 minutes) and learners must move from one 'island' to the next until all tasks are completed.

 Idea 4.5

Station-to-station

Move all tables to the edge of the classroom and create five or six 'stations' with different sets of source material (preferably photocopied in different colours) at each station. By each set of sources provide a list of questions that can be answered in 3 minutes. Allocate a group of learners to each station at the start of this activity. Ring a bell and ask each group to answer the questions before moving them on to the next 'station'. Move them around until all groups have answered the questions set. Times can be varied and different tasks/worksheets can be placed at each station. Inject a competitive air by offering a box of chocolates to the winning group.

Reducing the ratio of teacher talk to pupil talk

As teachers we often like the sound of our own voices and forget that many learners 'switch-off' after too much talking on our part. The following ideas will reduce the ratio of teacher/learner talk by setting up activities that allow students to figure out information rather than spoon-feeding this information to them.

 Idea 4.6

Snowball

Learners are asked to do an activity on their own for 5 minutes (for example, thinking of three questions they wish to ask about the subject studied). Learners pair up to answer their own questions. Learners are then formed into fours where they identify key issues, concepts, and so on that need to be explored further. Finally one member is chosen from each group to bring up issues/conclusions/suggestions that are useful for the class as a whole.

Best practice – avoid those sleepy corners!

- Avoid sleepy corners and the inertia that some students communicate by getting them used, from your very first lesson, to movement being a feature of your lessons.
- Add pace, dynamics and increased energy levels by regularly moving learners in your lessons.
- Make sure that in any group activity each learner is allocated a role (for example, scribe, orator, investigator etc). If each person in a group has a role and that role is necessary for the group you immediately negate much of the off-task behaviour that can be associated with 'group work' when it is badly deployed.

 Idea 4.7

Washing line banter

Clear the centre of the class so that you can create one long line of paired chairs that face each other. Along the centre of the line of chairs extend a piece of string with two contentious but opposing statements at each end of the washing line. Learners on one side of the room have to decide where they want to sit in relation to how far they agree or disagree with the statement. They then must justify to the person sitting opposite them why they have chosen to sit there. The job of the opposing person is convince them why they are wrong.

Idea 4.8

More dates please!

Produce one set of dates on A4 sheets of paper and provide a second sheet of dates with matching events. Give each learner either a date or an event and instruct them to find their counterpart in the classroom. Once all pairs have found each other, instruct them to line up against the wall of the classroom chronologically. Fire questions at named students to justify why they have chosen to stand where they have.

Idea 4.9

The eye of the storm!

Clear the centre of the classroom and place a cross (or, even better, a giant 'eye') in the centre of the classroom. Arrange chairs in a large circle around the 'eye' but at considerable distance from it. Ask for a volunteer to stand on the 'eye' and deliver a contentious statement related to the subject you are teaching. In turn, each learner has to stand up and move closer to or further from the eye, depending on if they agree or not, and defending to the class why they have chosen their position. Volunteers take it in turns to stand on the eye.

Idea 4.10

Catherine wheel!

Clear the centre of the classroom and arrange chairs in two concentric circles with each chair on the inside circle facing a chair on the outside. Learners take their seats facing each other and both talk for 2 minutes on a theme. Instruct the outer circle to move one place clockwise. The new talk-partners must first recount the content of the previous discussion before moving onto a new theme introduced by the teacher. After 2 more minutes move the outer circle as above and repeat the process with pairs summarizing all conversations that have taken place. This can be repeated as many times as the teacher sees fit.

Reflection point

In what ways do these teaching ideas help to differentiate lessons? Differentiation is about planning lessons and adapting teaching processes in order to meet the learning needs of all learners. Each learner is different due their education, psychology, learning style, physical characteristics, culture, gender, and so on. The strategies and ideas in this chapter automatically differentiate lessons by task (meeting their individual needs and learning styles by providing different audiences/activities for them to engage with) and by outcome (allowing different results and outcomes for different pupils according to activity).

 Idea 4.11

What/who am I?

This is a variation on a classic parlour game. Create packs of cards with key people/concepts/events (as fitting your subject) sufficient for a group of four or five learners. Place each pack face down in the middle of the table of each group. A 'player' picks a card to examine without showing it to the rest of the group. The rest of the group take turns in asking questions that can only be answered with a 'yes' or 'no'. Whoever guesses correctly chooses the next card and the game continues.

 Idea 4.12

Full house

Clear the centre of the classroom. Create one whole-class set of cards. Instead of 'suits' create cards that represent five or six different categories (for example, different professions, different political ideologies, different breeds of animals – whatever is appropriate for your subject). Within each category ensure that each card is different but represents something associated with that category (for example, a particular person, particular key concept, particular theory). Distribute one card to each learner. Their job is to find other learners associated with their category. Once all learners have found their respective groups, they then give a very short coherent presentation using each of the cards in their category.

Idea 4.13

Who wants to be a millionaire?

Based on the television quiz, this activity works well towards the end of any unit/module and requires the teacher to put two chairs at the front of the classroom. Give learners 10 minutes to create the quiz questions. If possible record the soundtrack of the show. Pick one learner to be the contestant and one to be the host, and use the questions that learners have created. Like the television show, give learners three 'lifelines': 50:50, phone a friend (ask someone in class) or ask the audience (everyone in the class writes an answer on a blank sheet of paper and holds it up). Swap the contestant and host.

 Reflection point

As teachers we often issue instructions without carefully reflecting on how important it is to break them down into manageable components. If you haven't already come across the acronym 'SMART' it stands for Specific, Measurable, Achievable, Realistic and Timed. The golden rule when carrying out any group-based active learning-strategies is that your instructions (and the activities that you require carried out) must be 'SMART'. Make sure that all instructions you issue can live up to this acronym.

 Idea 4.14

Anagram fun

This works well as a quick productive break between one section of the lesson and the next. Write a key phrase associated with the next phase of the lesson on the board. Ask learners to make as many words as they can from the title in 3 minutes.

 Idea 4.15

Kinaesthetic quiz

Using flashcards that you have prepared, put a pack of different coloured cards on each table. Each card contains information, for example, key terms, dates, images, and so on. Each table has 5 minutes to learn these before you remove

(Continued)

(Continued)

all the sources. Jigsaw the groups (see Idea 4.1) and then each learner explains their sources to another table. Reconvene the groups and set a competitive quiz based on all the sources with a prize for the winning group.

 Reflection point

How often can you hear a pin drop in your classroom? The chances are that if you are somebody that requires complete silence at home when concentrating, so will many of your learners. Silence, as a motivational teaching strategy, is very much underused by many teachers. However, if used skilfully it can provide a launchpad for productive and energized learner talk. In any active learning strategy that involves pair/group work it must be preceded by silent concentration (for example, reading and analysing, generating ideas). This short and rigorously policed period of silence will enhance the quality of learner talk that follows and provide a learning environment conducive to all your learners.

 Idea 4.16

Blame the DJ!

Put together a CD of 12 songs related to the subject you are teaching. Edit down to 5 seconds for each song (intros are best). The class, arranged into teams, has to guess the group/song title or both. Offer a prize for the winners and use the themes within the songs to launch the next section of your lesson.

Best practice – activity scaffolding

Practitioners have found it effective to consider:

- When deploying group-based activities keep momentum, pace and dynamics at a maximum by reconfiguring the groups. This helps to avoid attention spans drifting and off-task banter developing by refocusing the task in hand with a new group of learners.
- Ensuring that when moving learners to the next group there is a different task to carry out and one that is contingent on the participation of all members of the newly formed group.

- When carrying out complex movement of learners in your class project a 'map' or 'plan' to show where in the room learners are to go. If creating 'stations' or learner hotspots, make sure that these are clearly labelled on the walls or the tables that learners are to go to. Use brightly coloured paper for labels/ resources that help distinguish one 'hotspot' from another.
- When moving learners keep instructions short, clear and slow and, where appropriate, accompany each set of instructions with a timed target.

Questions for professional development

1. Do you know who the excellent practitioners are in the institution you teach in? Find out who these teachers are and talk to them and, if possible, observe them. Glean from them any advice and guidance that you can incorporate into your own lessons.
2. Are you aware of which areas of your own practice you feel you are weakest in (for example, the deployment of resources, use of questioning strategies, the use of group based learning strategies, and so on)? Draw up a wish list of what you would like to improve and talk to other members of staff to find out which teachers excel in these areas and observe their praxis.
3. Have you ever volunteered to have trainee teachers observe your own lessons? Preparing for any observation enables you to reflect on and evaluate your own practice, and often forces you to be more creative and imaginative. Talking through these activities with the observer afterwards often throws an invaluable spotlight on how you can take your own practice forward.
4. Do you ever give your learners an opportunity to evaluate your teaching? Create an evaluation sheet (this can include the names of modules taught and so on, but it can also include various teaching strategies you deploy, seating arrangements in class, and so on). Use this information to inform future planning and orchestration of your lessons.

Checklist: building your toolbox

- Set the tone and high expectations of the lesson by capturing the imagination of learners at the start. The use of a very few seconds of film footage can pay dividends if this is the right film clip, particularly if you can make conceptual links back to the film clip throughout the lesson.
- Avoid using threats and undue pressure when carrying out complex activities. Providing this is carefully managed, learning is always more productive when learners are having fun.

- Never underestimate the importance of the classroom environment on learner motivation. Classrooms that look run-down, with tatty posters and peeling wallpaper, can convey low expectations on the part of the teacher of their learners. Buy pot plants, invest in new posters, put up colourful key words and concepts, get rid of broken chairs, and so on. All these actions will convey care, professionalism and an enthusiasm for your learners and the subject.
- Establishing a rapport with learners is key to successful teaching and learning. Concentrate on giving eye contact to all learners when teaching; make sure that body postures do not 'exclude' (for example, avoid folded arms, hands on hips); and make sure that praise is sensibly and appropriate given, and is backed up with a warm smile.
- Ensure that learners see the relevance of what they are learning to their own lives, biographies and so on. If using complex concepts or referring to periods in history, use analogies/metaphors/examples that bring the concept 'alive' to teenagers today.

Chapter links

The ideas in this chapter relate closely with those also explored in Chapters 1, 2, 5, 6 and 8.

Further reading

Gilbert, I. (2002) *Essential Motivation in the Classroom*. London: Routledge/Falmer.
This excellent bite-sized book applies a range of motivational theories to teaching, learning and thinking in the classroom.

CHAPTER 5

BUILDING AN EFFECTIVE CLIMATE

Chapter overview

The aims of the chapter are to:

1. Illustrate ways in which you can foster a learning climate through pace, questioning and cooperative work.
2. Suggest practical ideas and activities for the structuring of cooperative and peer learning opportunities.
3. Provide guidance on the use of effective feedback for learning.
4. Provide ideas for the use of self-assessment techniques as a basis for learner motivation.

Problem-solving

In this chapter, we consider how to construct a motivating climate in the classroom. In doing so, we recognize the difficulties in getting learners to cooperate with one another and the challenges facing teachers and learners alike of collaborative learning, self-assessment and the pitching and recording of feedback on learning.

Successful and effective teaching and learning are always collaborative in nature. Learners need to collaborate both with each other and with the teacher if a sustainable and motivating learning atmosphere is to be developed. Student-centred teaching and learning (a clumsy description, and, in a real sense, how can learning not be student centred?), as opposed to more 'didactic' methods of teacher delivery, are usually seen to be more engaging and sustainable over longer periods of time. Yet perhaps they are harder to set up and manage at first? They certainly involve very careful planning.

By 'climate' we refer to the 'learning atmosphere'. This is a subtle and often difficult and slippery notion to pin down. Having said this, take a walk through the corridors of a school or college and take a peek inside the various rooms you find. Some lessons – as social encounters – seem to 'just work right'; there is clearly learning taking place, learners (and teachers) are enjoying the activities and each others' company, and the work and pace are productive. Often such classrooms are noisy – we believe that learning (and especially cooperative learning) is noisy, and classrooms and educational environments are all the better for it! This observation might even challenge your notions of what effective teaching and learning look and sound like?

Within this climate, learners need to feel that the work they do has value and that they can see themselves learning step by step. There is nothing less motivating than feeling your learning is standing still.

Context

The claim of much research to have come from the Assessment Reform Group (2002b) is that feedback and appropriately scheduled and managed peer assessment, collaborative learning and self-assessment are themselves highly motivating: it is essential for learner engagement that those we teach feel they are moving forwards and gaining success. Many of the ideas in this chapter deal with tools for getting learners working together and cooperating as a means to create the required climate leading to productive learning. We tend, thanks to the work of the Assessment Reform Group, to make an important distinction between assessment for learning and assessment of learning. The work of this group (2002b) suggests that learners need to understand where they are in their learning journey – they need to see clearly the distance they have travelled, and what they have left to do. Most importantly, they need to see how to get to the next step in their learning. Thus, we need to teach and provide feedback which directly enables learners to become engaged, see the point, want to be involved and understand their own learning processes.

Alongside the importance of 'teaching for motivation' is the observation that classroom spaces where learners are motivated have a very rich and distinctive atmosphere. While drawing upon a primary sector example, the 2000 Hay McBer report has attempted to characterize 'effective practice' for primary classrooms. This report argues that there are three key features which combine in numerous ways to affect pupil progress (in their learning). These dimensions of learning are:

- teaching skills;
- professional characteristics;
- classroom climate.

What is significant about this is the notion that these three dimensions of effective teaching are actually 'within the control of the teacher to affect and change'. Thus, although the report openly recognizes that 'teachers are not clones', none the less, classroom and learning climate is seen as an essential means through which we can affect learners and their learning. In this research report, climate is defined as how it 'feels' for learners to be 'in a particular teacher's classroom', and what this then does to the motivation of those learners.

Toolbox

Climate-building ideas

In this chapter we look at some simple ideas for engaging learners, getting them talking, encouraging them to ask and answer questions, and the role played by feedback in engaging learners further. In this way, all the ideas in this chapter can go some way to developing a motivating 'climate' in your classroom.

 Idea 5.1

A picture speaks a thousand words . . . and communicates your ethos

At a mid-point in the year/programme/course try to get learners to write how they feel about their learning and their progression. Encourage them to communicate to a readership of next year's learners the enjoyments and challenges

(Continued)

(Continued)

of your subject/class/teaching. With appropriate ethical permissions, take pictures of learners and turn these into colourful head and shoulders posters with the quotations to display in your classroom and at parents' evenings and open-day events. Capture the learners speaking about what they like and enjoy, and set up the next set of learners to see how they too might be engaged and be successful. Do not underestimate the power of having your picture and your own words displayed back to you and the group – it really validates for the learners the respect and value the teacher places on them and their learning.

 Idea 5.2

State your intentions clearly

Make sure that every lesson starts with an absolutely clear indication of what the aims are, but also what the point of the learning is. Many teachers do the first but sometimes forget to do the second. This is really important for scene-setting and climate development and it also helps with wider 'assessment for learning' strategies (see Chapter 3).

For example, you could start lessons with the following four-segment piece of communication:

1. The aims of today's lesson are to . . .
2. Firstly, we are going to . . ., secondly, you will . . ., and thirdly, we will all . . .
3. The way we will assess our learning today is by . . .
4. Finally, the point of today's lesson is . . .

Best practice – aims and objectives

Practitioners have found it effective to consider:

- How aims and objectives are expressed.
- How we can get our learners to make sense of the language we use to express our aims and objectives.
- How we might get learners to document the aims of the lesson and the aims of their learning for their future reference.
- How learners see the connections between past, current and future lessons.

- How we make assessment opportunities clear to learners at the start of lessons.
- How to 'draw together' the learners at the end of a lesson and get each individual to articulate and/or record what they think they have learnt.

Idea 5.3

Aiming precisely

However you make clear the aims and objectives of the lesson to your learners (see Idea 5.2), it is a good idea to encourage your learners to 'own' them by rephrasing these aims in their own words (by saying or writing them). This is so that they can both understand them and communicate back to you that they understand them. This is important and useful for climate-setting since it shows learners that the point of the lesson (and their behaviour) is their own participation in the learning process. Thus, learning is not something 'done to them' but something they have an investment in.

The role of 'talk' in the classroom

The following suggestions and strategies are based upon the simple – but effective – notion that getting learners to speak out loud in the session really adds to the 'feel' of the overall classroom experience in a very positive way.

Idea 5.4

It's good to talk

Using very low-level learning (recalling, listing, defining, remembering) you can encourage all learners to say something in the first few minutes of the lesson. You can simply assess prior learning by getting all learners to list something they already remember and have learnt previously. Get everyone talking – ask questions and for contributions from everyone, and try to get everyone saying something. Asking everyone to speak (and getting them used to this over time) leads to learners being willing to participate and really helps climate-setting since it is a massive statement about what you want from them in the lesson – their learning and their participation. You might do this before you move onto the 'aims of the lesson' in a formal sense.

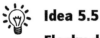

Idea 5.5

Flashy definitions

Another way to encourage all learners to speak within the first few minutes of a lesson is to get them to define terms, ideas, things from 'flash cards' that you have prepared. Get A4 paper (coloured if you have it) and print out as large as possible the technical and specialist vocabularies from your subject specialism. You might even laminate the cards to ensure you can reuse them each year in good condition. You can play 'choose the card, any card . . .' with learners, asking them to tell you something about the thing identified on the flash card. Do this with pace and the 'surprise' element of the random choice of card and learners really respond well. A good way to start (and end) lessons.

Idea 5.6

A wall of words

Following on from the creation of your flash cards (see Idea 5.5 above) you can use the same cards as a simple but highly effective wall display. Print out all the words/terms/names/case studies of your subject matter (every subject has these at every level) and post them up on walls and ceilings! You can even colour-code certain modules/subjects/themes within the cards you have made. This colourful display often engages learners – it makes the technical language of your subject come alive – and you can use it as a teaching tool.

 Reflection point

If you wish to engage your learners and make them feel welcomed and excited in your classroom, then think about the environment you work within. Can you greet them at the door (this personal contact makes such a genuine difference)? What can you display on notice boards and walls which will help them? Can you display on a board forthcoming homework if they wish to get a head start, or show them useful websites for their support and revision?

Thinking skills

Another way to develop the learning climate or atmosphere you want is to encourage the development of 'thinking skills' (see Chapter 12 for further ideas). Getting learners to think, articulate their thoughts and evaluate is quite 'motivating' once these very same learners see the changes taking place in their own cognitive abilities.

 Idea 5.7

Thinking through the subject's shoes

If you teach a subject that contains different views, cases, characters, genres, theories or approaches, you can ask learners to try each different 'hat' on for size. Get them to write in the language and style of the different aspects of their specialist curriculum as if they themselves were an expert thinking it. This writing can be posted up on your walls. When we tried this idea, learners were so pleased and proud with what they had written and that their name was on the classroom wall that they sometimes (in secret) brought their friends in to see their work!

 Idea 5.8

Power lists

Do not underestimate the power and discipline to be had through exercising learners' memories as a 'warm-up' at the start of the lesson. Get learners making lists (maybe in silence), comparing lists, and defining each others' words. Very soon such low-level recall techniques can lead to excellent ongoing revision but also great opportunities for social and collaborative learning; once they all have lists and compare with their partner, and define and test each other, you have them all interacting at the start of the lesson. You can then continue with the right interactive atmosphere in place.

 Reflection point

The notion of list-making is a very simple and powerful revision strategy. Although a relatively low-order skill (recall), you can help learners to really gain confidence and focus through repeating list-making exercises. Try to apply this

(Continued)

(Continued)

to your own subject specialism. What lists could learners draw up? At what points in the sequence of your scheme of work would it make sense to get learners to review and list their prior learning? How can you maximize these opportunities to ensure that when new knowledge comes, it can be built onto the foundation of the old learning in as secure a way as possible?

Idea 5.9
Thinking time

This is a well-known and highly successful recommendation to come out of the large body of research into 'assessment for learning' (see Chapters 3 and 9). When asking questions – especially at the very start of the session before learners might be 'settled-in' or 'warmed-up' – it is often hard to get some learners confidently talking. Often it is the case that you might get the same learners answering each time. Avoid both these issues through the introduction of 'thinking time' – a little pause where you ask the class to think of an answer before you then ask the question a second time. After all, if you rapid-fire questions 'cold', what are you really testing? Are you testing their knowledge or their reaction time and confidence? (These are not the same.) The thinking time approach allows time for more considered and thoughtful answers and is itself motivating since learners are able to participate.

Idea 5.10
'Think, Pair, Share'

This is another variation on the 'thinking-time approach' as identified in Idea 5.9 above. It is also an 'assessment for learning' strategy which is linked to increased learner motivation. When asking a question of the group, ask for some 'thinking time' (as above). But then, ask learners to bounce their answers off each other in pairs before finally settling on hearing contributions from learners to the whole group. Thus, in three steps they have:

1. thought during some thinking time;
2. had the chance to compare and share ideas with a partner;
3. had the chance to feedback to the whole group and hear a wide range of contributions.

This is a good and easy cooperative learning strategy and also is very motivating since learners are not 'caught out' or paralysed by sudden unexpected questions. An extension of this for group work is the 'buzz group' approach.

Idea 5.11
Peer riffing

When eliciting responses from learners – especially if you are asking them to recall things they have learnt previously – a useful technique is to 'bounce' or 'riff' answers into the next question and so on. For example, one learner gives an answer to a question, you then ask the next learner 'what does that mean?'. You then link words from the answer to this question into the next question, and so on. For example, a student uses a key phrase in their answer to you, and so you take this key phrase and use it as the next question – you could ask 'What does XXX mean?' or 'Can you give me an example of XXX?'. In this way the answers link to the next question and you can build up a good pace and flow. This has a number of positive effects: you can get learners listening to each other more easily; it injects pace into the lesson; you can develop a really productive climate where learners are manipulating knowledge and language with the teacher simply organizing and orchestrating opportunities between the learners for them to speak.

Assessment and climate

If pitched correctly, assessment methods should be a means through which you can further engage learners – and, once more, build an ethos where learners are receptive, willing to make mistakes and want feedback.

Idea 5.12
Medal and mission feedback

The 'Inside the Black Box' research (see Black et al., 2003) advocates the medal and mission style of feedback as a highly motivating technique for assessment for learning. In this method, grades are often withheld and formative assessment

(Continued)

(Continued)

is marked with a description of 'medals' (things learners have done well) and 'missions' – the next steps for the learner to undertake to improve the learning further. In this way, feedback becomes 'feedforward'; learners become clear as to what are the next steps of their learning. This is seen to be a highly motivating form of assessment, and is the first step towards more 'meta-cognitive' thinking (see Chapter 12) where learners are able to self-assess their own thinking processes and strategies. We often call this self-assessment ipsative assessment. For a fuller discussion of assessment for motivation see Chapters 2, 3 and 9.

 Reflection point

Think about what you might need to do to get medal and mission feedback accepted by your colleagues, your learners and the institution as a whole. Are you in a position where you are able to stop grading? Does this conflict with wider institutional policies? How might learners first respond to the medal and mission strategy if you adopted it? How would you need to warn them and explain to them what you are doing?

 Idea 5.13

Pitch the reward clearly

It is often too easy for teachers to make unthinking 'rewards' of learners' contributions. It is all too easy to say 'well done' or even 'excellent' to learners for contributions which are not actually excellent in themselves. This is because when saying 'well done' (for finding something to say) we actually mean something like 'thank you for answering', which is not what we say, and means something quite different. Be really careful about this. If you wish your learners to be motivated, then do not offer empty praise which ultimately, over time, will become a devalued and reduced currency.

Try instead to say 'thank you', if that is what you actually mean. If the verbal contribution is indeed 'very good', then you need to clarify to the learner and to the rest of the group exactly why the contribution was good. However, you need to do this as succinctly as possible. For example, you could say: 'Very good. It was excellent how you used the key words there – exactly the language you need to use in your exam.' This makes everyone completely clear what you are rewarding and why and so this is much more motivating since it helps learners be clear on their progress and on your standards.

Idea 5.14

Using plenaries for ipsative assessment

Make the most of those last 5–10 minutes of the lesson. The end is just as important as the start. Plan activities which encourage and enable learners to say what they have done and what they have learnt. Get them to also tell you what they think they need to do next or might need some more help with. This is highly motivating – providing you are then actually seen to respond to what they have said. This ipsative assessment (self-assessment, looking into the future) could be verbalized, shared in pairs, written down, and so on.

Idea 5.15

'Ticket out of the door'

At the end of your lesson give learners a final quick task, the completion of which acts as their ticket or pass out of the door. You can use this opportunity for peer assessment or self-assessment. This really affects the climate of the lesson – it shows just how responsive you are to your learners and how much they can recognize they have learnt. Allow them to leave knowing what they have done and learnt. They will, over time, recognize the effectiveness of classes with you and come to trust you and enjoy their learning with you.

Idea 5.16

Role of choice

Choice is often something we do not give our learners enough of. With appropriate opportunities for self-assessment and target setting (and maybe in conjunction with 'medal and mission' style feedback (see Idea 5.12)) we can ask learners to choose what learning they do. They could choose materials, the order they do things or even how much help they allow themselves to have while working on a task. Giving choice creates such a positive climate and learners tend to respond well as long as the choices are framed and supported appropriately.

Best practice – choice

Practitioners have found it effective to consider:

- How to guide learners to frame their choices appropriately.
- How to use choice as a means to differentiate.
- When to provide opportunities for choice on a scheme of work.
- What choice might mean for the dynamics of planning and teaching the lesson in question – does this mean everyone doing different things and how does the teacher manage this?
- How to ensure that within choice, learners still stretch and challenge themselves.
- Learners do not choose impossible tasks which demotivate.

 Idea 5.17

The honesty box

The honesty box is, literally, a box into which you ask your learners to admit to things they do not know but feel they probably should. This way anonymity is ensured – learners just put questions confidentially into the box – and teachers (and learners) can then deal with the issues and questions with the whole class at another time. Getting the class to answer its own questions also creates a very collaborative atmosphere. This technique could be used as the 'ticket out of the door' (see Idea 5.15).

Questions for professional development

1. How would you describe the most productive and effective learning climate you have constructed? What were the learners doing and how did their actions contribute to the climate as a whole? How can you re-create this climate and make it sustainable?
2. How can you structure into your lesson planning and scheme of work design significant opportunities for ipsative and peer assessment and feedback? Where would these be best placed in the overall sequence and how would you communicate the feedback to your learners? (See Chapter 9 for further advice on this.)
3. What rewards are there for learners to learn in your class? How do you make success, learning, effort, application and challenge their own reward? How do you communicate this to your learners so it makes sense to them?
4. How will you greet/set the tone for each new class the first time you meet them? How will you communicate your expectations so they can understand and see the need to work and apply themselves? How can you communicate to them your expectations of a learning atmosphere?

Checklist: building your toolbox

- Plan peer assessment, individual assessment and self-assessment opportunities with the resulting feedback as a formal element on your scheme of work. Really try and give these opportunities significant and discrete priority.
- Ensure you always communicate to learners what the point of their learning is. Do this at the start and the end of lessons, and ask them to relate back to you this information in their own words. In this way they will understand the learning journey they are on.
- Develop a variety of ways for learners to understand the aims of lessons without you simply telling them at the start of each lesson. Get them to be clear in their own words what the point of the learning is and how it links to previous (and future) lessons.
- Develop your own clear sets of phrases to communicate praise. Do not just end every learner contribution with 'excellent' but keep your praise only for when 'excellent' answers really are 'excellent'.
- Develop strategies for getting learners to speak within the first few minutes of every lesson.
- Start your planning by always asking yourself the questions 'What will learners be doing?' and 'How will this task/sequence engage and capture them?' Plan teaching for motivation from the start.
- Use wall displays to illustrate to learners that you value their work.
- Develop a series of low-order, fast-paced starter activities to set the pace of the session as you mean to go on.
- Always find time at the end of a lesson to ask learners what they have learnt and what they need more help with.

Chapter links

The ideas in this chapter relate closely with those also explored in Chapters 1, 2, 3 and 6.

Further reading

See Chapter 3 in this book, on assessment for motivation – this picks up on some of the ideas and tools raised here. You also might wish to refer to the chapters on assessment and on motivation in our other Sage textbook, *Successful Teaching 14–19: Theory, Practice and Reflection* (Kidd and Czerniawski, 2010).

Assessment Reform Group (2002) *Testing, Motivation and Learning*. Cambridge: University of Cambridge. See this for a wider discussion of the role to be played by ipsative and peer assessment and feedback in engaging learners.

CHAPTER 6

STRATEGIES FOR COOPERATIVE AND SOCIAL LEARNING

Chapter overview

The aims of the chapter are to:

1. Offer seating strategies designed to encourage social learning.
2. Provide suggestions to enhance peer working practices.
3. Enable conditions in which successful group work can take place.
4. Provide advice and guidance on how best to encourage classroom discussion.

Problem-solving

This chapter reinforces the notion that for successful classroom teaching, we firmly believe that focused and challenging classroom 'talk' is an essential component to mixed-ability teaching. Not only can this enthuse learners and boost their confidence, but it also provides a rich environment for teachers to monitor, assess and encourage any transition from surface to deep learning. Successful classroom discussion, 'group work' and the interplay between the two are not things that can just be thrown together on a whim. Both require careful planning, orchestration and conducting on the part of the teacher. We passionately believe that noisy classrooms are classrooms where successful learning is taking place, providing the teacher manages and harnesses student interaction. In Chapters 2 and 5 we introduced you to a variety of ways to establish group dynamics. It is important to break down barriers as quickly as possible so that you can create the right sort of classroom dynamics for successful learning to take place. It is also important for your learners to see you confidently manipulating the classroom in imaginative and creative ways. Your confidence in doing this will enable and encourage your learners to believe in the learning outcomes of each strategy you deploy. This includes the classroom space in which you operate. For this reason, the chapter devotes considerable time to the variety of ways you can deploy classroom furniture to enhance the learning experience of your students.

Context

By 'active learning' we include classroom strategies that engage learners through talk and peer interaction. These strategies are often rooted in a theoretical base of constructivism (Piaget, 1950; Wertsch, 1997) and often help learners to develop higher-order evaluation skills through learning and discovering together. The constructivist approach is concerned with the processes of learning and the role of the learner in particular. It assumes that there are no such things as 'facts' in that all facts, scientific or otherwise, are socially constructed in the first place. Knowledge is therefore assumed to be constructed by learners themselves and learning is seen as an active process of construction and knowledge accumulation. The teacher is viewed as a 'facilitator' of active learning. Learners 'restructure' what they see and hear, think and rethink ideas until 'personal meanings' are formed. This pedagogic approach assumes that mistakes are an essential part of the learning process providing learners talk, solve problems, make decisions and form opinions. In this sense, knowledge does not exist separately from the knower, but is only 'made sense of' through learners interacting with the objects of their learning, building meaning and sense-making. Value is therefore placed on the variety of active learning that learners take up along with the facilitator role that the teacher occupies. It should be stressed that this particular school of learning is one of many, but it is at the core of most of the ideas you will read in this chapter. However, unless classroom talk is tightly managed it can quickly dissolve into low- (and sometimes high-) level off-task behaviour. The ideas in this chapter will enable you to energize the classroom and provide all learners with the opportunity to engage in targeted conversation. By experimenting with new seating you will energize your teaching space and create new opportunities for cooperative and social learning, affording learners the opportunity for greater recall, as and when they require this information. This provision of deep learning will provide you with invaluable opportunities to monitor and evaluate to what extent your teaching has been successful.

Toolbox

Experimenting with new seating arrangements

The professional layout of the room should convery the very same professional values that you communicate to your learners. As such it is a vital tool in the repertoire of classroom management strategies. We fully realize that in many cases you will not be lucky enough to have your own 'base-room' and this makes it more difficult to arrange the classroom to match individual learning objectives. However, lessons that start at the beginning of the day, just after break or after lunch do provide the opportunity for tables to be moved, chairs to be rearranged and so on. Whether you have a base-room or not there should be a 'wow' factor when learners enter your teaching space. We present 10 ways that you can organize your teaching area to maximize classroom management and get the most out of the creative teaching strategies you deploy. These teaching strategies are based on three principles. First, the teacher needs to be able to make eye contact with all learners. Second, the teacher should be able to move freely around the room so he or she can move closer to all learners as needed. Third, seating should be 'fit-for-purpose', that is, it matches the activities planned for the lesson. Always remember to ask permission before moving anything in somebody else's teaching space.

Idea 6.1
Horseshoe teaching space

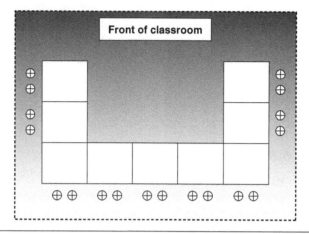

Figure 6.1 Horseshoe teaching space

Arrange the desks and chairs as a large U-shape facing the front of the classroom. This allows the teacher to be the central focus in the classroom while encouraging discussion between peers, since all learners can see each other. The teacher can move around the group easily (remember to allow sufficient space for teacher movement around the outside of the U-shape as well as inside). Learners can also move their chairs to the inside of the U-shape to create smaller working groups if necessary.

Idea 6.2
Diamonds

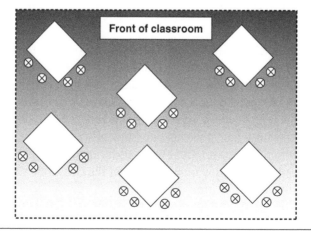

Figure 6.2 Diamonds

(Continued)

(Continued)

Arrange the tables in diamond formations of four learners but with the seating placed so that all learners can see the board and the teacher. This particular seating arrangement allows students to see the board at all times, facilitates easy teacher mobility and enables more advanced group-based strategies where learners are required to move from one table to another.

 Idea 6.3

Flush to the wall

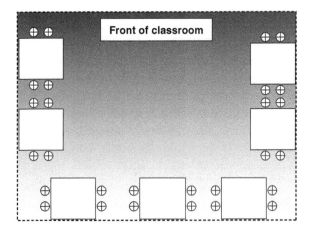

Figure 6.3   Flush to the wall

We often hear teachers saying 'my classroom is too small to do group work'. You will be amazed at how much space you can create by simply moving the tables flush against the wall. As a classroom management strategy this has the effect of opening up considerable space in the centre of the class while, at the same time, allowing you to stand between groups when teaching. This is really useful when policing potential off-task inter-table banter. The gaps between tables are also ideal when using questioning strategies, allowing the teacher to move easily from one part of the classroom to the next, firing questions at individuals or groups.

Idea 6.4

Circle seating with breakout tables for group work

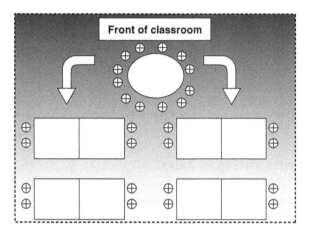

Figure 6.4   Circle seating with breakout tables for group work

Arrange the table and chairs (this can also be done without the table) in a circle towards the front of the class. Have a second formation of tables arranged in groups. With these two distinct areas the teacher can provide an opening dialogue, sets of instructions, and so on. Alternatively, students can brainstorm ideas before setting off to work on these ideas in smaller groups. Learners can also return to the circle for plenary work.

Best practice – factors to consider when using new seating arrangements

Creating excellent group dynamics is more than just a matter of moving tables. The following points need to be considered when creating new seating arrangements:

- Prevent learners who habitually communicate off task from sitting opposite each other.
- When speaking to learners, simply kneeling down or crouching sends out a subtle yet powerful message that you are communicating at the level of the

(Continued)

(Continued)

learner and that you are conscious about potential differences in the power and status of teacher and learner.

- Consider and experiment with the make-up of each group, for example, gender, mixed ability, extroverts, when developing group dynamics.
- Leave sufficient space between chairs and tables for easy movement of teachers and learners.

Idea 6.5

Students sitting in pairs

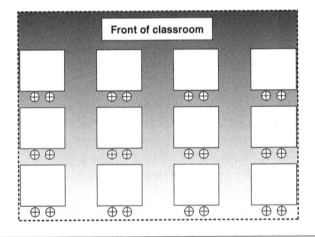

Figure 6.5   Students sitting in pairs

Arrange tables in pairs remembering to make sure that you can work easily between the pairs. All too often paired seating arrangements in classrooms are replaced by rows restricting the ability of the teacher to move between learners. Rowed seating makes it harder for any teacher to pre-empt off-task behaviour (for example, members of row in front learning back to chat with those behind). Paired seating is ideal when getting learners to focus and maximise task-related discussions. This strategy is also ideal when taking over new classes where behaviour management might be an issue.

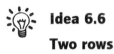 **Idea 6.6**

Two rows

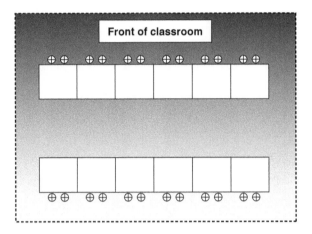

Figure 6.6   Two rows

Arrange the tables in two lines with chairs arranged so that learners face each other. Place sufficient space between the two rows of tables so that a spacious area in the centre of the class is created. This table arrangement is useful for whole-classroom debates and other active learning strategies where you might wish students to come to the centre of the class (for example, role plays, games). This is particularly useful when a competitive element is required as part of the pace and dynamics of the lesson structure.

 Reflection point

Where is the teacher's desk and why does it need to be there? Why do you need it at all? All too often it is located at the front of the class and takes up valuable teaching and learning space (often encouraging the teacher to stand, or sit, at the front of the class instead of moving around). If you do not need the desk, then move it. Slide it to the side of a wall or under the smartboard (if you have one). The extra space created can be used to enhance the teaching area, enabling you to experiment with different seating arrangements.

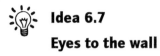

Idea 6.7

Eyes to the wall

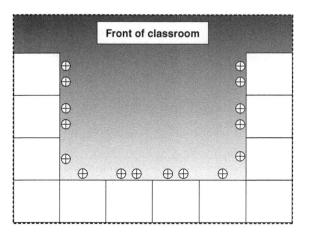

Figure 6.7 Eyes to the wall

At first glance this particular seating arrangement looks like anything but social. In fact, it is a powerful tool for classroom discussion if utilized well. Arrange tables so that they are flush to the wall in the shape of a giant-U. This arrangement works really well when students need time to concentrate and immerse themselves in reading or problem-solving activities. This position means that learners are not easily distracted and gives a sense of gravitas to any activity. By asking learners to turn their chairs around to face you and their colleagues it is easy to ask questions and to generate whole-class discussions based on the high-intensity learning they have just experienced.

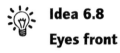

Idea 6.8

Eyes front

Arrange tables in V-formations facing the front of the class. Ideally no more than four students should be allocated to their 'V'. This particular arrangement is ideal for group work and means that the front of the classroom is visible at all times

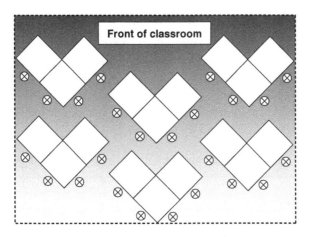

Figure 6.8   Eyes Front

to learners. It provides a semi-private space for the teacher to work with each group while powerfully conveying a sense of purpose as learners enter the classroom for the first time.

Best practice – creating the 'wow' factor

However much effort you put into your lesson plans to make your teaching stand out from the crowd, it is important to remember that students are coming and going from classrooms all day long. Moving chairs and tables in an attempt to generate cooperative and social learning will help, but it is not enough. Your professional values and high expectations of them and your own practice will dictate what sort of environment they respond to. This means that you should ensure in every lesson that:

- Any wall/ceiling displays look presentable (always carry some reusable adhesive with you).
- You scan the room quickly before any lesson starts and get rid of plastic bottles, crisps packets, and so on.
- You note broken cupboard doors, non-functioning blinds, and so on, and notify your technician.
- You make sure that books, pens, rubbers, and so on are displayed neatly and labelled (for example, provide colour codes, book ends).

(Continued)

(Continued)

- Any resources prepared or used by you look professional and aesthetically pleasing (with today's word-processing packages there is no excuse for boring and dull handouts).
- You make sure that chairs and tables are not scattered around haphazardly but are arranged 'fit for purpose' before students come into your teaching area.

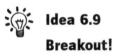

Idea 6.9

Breakout!

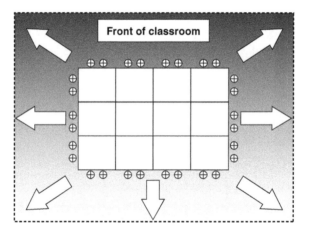

Figure 6.9   Breakout!

Arrange seating so that all tables in the centre of the room have learners seated around the perimeter. The main focus of this sort of lesson will not be the tables in the centre but, rather, the space you create around the edges of your class-room. These spaces can be used for separate kinaesthetic activities in different parts of the classroom (for example, designated areas where students have to test each other on a topic before moving to the next designated area). The table area can be used to brief and convene the class at various stages of the lesson. If the tables are not needed, then they can be stacked on top of each other while activities are taking place.

Idea 6.10

Examination practice

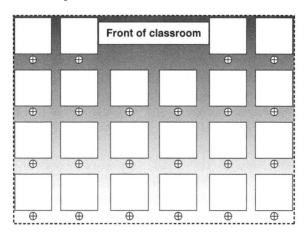

Figure 6.10   Examination practice

Strictly speaking this table arrangement is not ideal for social learning, however we have included this as an essential seating arrangement when getting learners used to public and formal assessments. The individual separation of learners that restricts social interaction can be balanced with adept questioning strategies on the part of the teacher to generate whole-classroom discussion after any practice assessment exercise.

Best practice – when the tables and chairs cannot be moved

For many colleagues teaching in specialist classrooms (IT rooms, science laboratories, workshops, and so on) opportunities to rearrange teaching spaces might appear less possible. Tables and workstations might be fixed or too heavy and sockets/plugs/pipes might impede furniture arrangements and mobility. When teaching in such rooms, consider the 10 diagrams above and reflect upon the opportunities and challenges these spaces provide. For example, many science laboratories most closely resemble Figures 6.2 and 6.8 (with careful placing of chairs). On the other hand, IT workstations might resemble Figure 6.6 and/or Figure 6.7. Irrespective of whether the tables can or cannot be moved, it is important to remember that the learners (and in many cases, their stools/chairs) can! It is perfectly possible to re-create the spirit of Figures 6.4, 6.8 and 6.9 even if learners are asked to stand up and move to the front of the class at key moments in the flow of the lesson.

Developing peer working practices and cooperative learning

Peer working practices refer to those processes whereby young people undertake informal or formal educational activities with their peers, that is, those that share similarities to themselves in age, educational/socio-economic background, interests, and so on. A variety of theories underpin peer working strategies. For example, Fishbein and Ajzen's (1975) theory of reasoned action states that the intention of a person to adopt a recommended behaviour is determined by a person's subjective and normative beliefs about the outcome of their behaviour. Bandura's (2006) social learning theory is based on the idea that people learn best through direct experience and by observing and modelling the behaviour of others with whom that person identifies. These and many other theories argue that peer working practices are effective because young learners' attitudes are highly influenced by the perception of what their peers do and think. To develop peer working practices we encourage the use of a range of active learning strategies, including brainstorming, small-group/pair discussions, games, quizzes and role plays.

 Reflection point

When considering pace and dynamics in your teaching, it is really helpful to reflect on the difference between ice-breakers and energizers (YPeer, 2005). Ice-breakers are used at the beginning of courses or new units/modules to help people feel at ease, whereas energizers are activities used to stimulate and motivate learners during particular sessions, especially when attention levels might be sagging (very common on Friday afternoons or for sessions being taught in the evening). Energizers often involve kinaesthetic (involving movement) activities and can be deployed when learners are looking sleepy, as a powerful transition point between one phase of the lesson and the next or as a way of introducing a new topic. Try to avoid making them too long and move swiftly on to the next activity once you have 'energized' your audience.

 Idea 6.11

Debating pairs

This activity is a great 'energizer' and particularly useful if attention levels are in danger of dropping or if sessions are of a longer than normal duration. Tables are not used in this activity so move them, if possible, to the side of the teaching area. Arrange chairs in pairs but so that each chair faces each other in one long row down the length of the class. Choose two articles that offer opposing views on an issue and give one article to one half of the pair and one to the other. Allow learners time to read the article and a further 5 minutes to prepare their case. They now have 5 minutes to debate furiously with the person sitting opposite them. Once done, move half the pairs clockwise and repeat the debating activity. Each repetition will hone their understanding of the topic and develop their own point of view within existing debates.

Idea 6.12

From our own correspondent

This activity fosters communication, research and peer working skills. Set up stations around the classroom that contain resources related to your subject area (for example, photographs, artefacts, newspaper articles). Divide the class into groups of four or five learners, all with the objective to understand all aspects of the topic exhibited around the room. One learner from each group is sent to each area of the classroom (jigsaw) where they work with other group representatives to unpack all the relevant information at the particular station they have been sent to. Feeling clear and confident about their particular area, they go back to their home groups and explain their findings, with home group members writing down (works best if they are given a pro forma to work to) all relevant information.

Idea 6.13

Question relay

Make up a box or basket in which you have put lots of questions on strips of paper. Split the class into small groups. One member from each group runs to the front to get a question and goes back to the group to confer. When they have conferred, he or she returns to the teacher and explains the answer. If it is correct, the runner picks out the next question; if it is incorrect, the runner returns to the group to confer. The winning group is the group that answers the most questions.

Reflection point

Revision periods are often the most enjoyable phases of the teaching year. In most cases, learners have covered all the material and should have some understanding of most of it. Their motivation levels will be heightened as they draw nearer to final assessment. This is a great opportunity for you to introduce a range of fun activities that get learners, in their peer groups, to identify examination-based skills.

 Idea 6.14

Exambuster

This activity is a highly effective examination revision strategy. Arrange the classroom in grouped table formations with flip-chart paper and marker pens on each table. Divide the class up so that (ideally) pairs/threes can move and work on one table at any time (this can work with up to four learners but no more). On each flip-chart sheet write down an examination-based question, making sure a different question is on each table and written at the top of the sheet. The objective is to make sure that all students answer all questions laid out before them. At the word 'go' each group attempts to answer the question on their table. After 5 minutes, move students on to the next table. This time their job is to add/delete/edit what has been written, the aim being to produce the perfect answer. This activity continues until all questions have been attempted. Once back at their home group, students can be given a simplified mark scheme to mark the final answer laid out before them – the sum contributions of the whole class.

 Idea 6.15

Post haste!

This is another simple but very effective examination revision strategy where cooperative learning plays a significant role. Give each group of between three and five learners a theme to summarize. Ask each member of the group to then summarize one point on a Post-it note. All Post-it notes are displayed around the class and learners then copy down the material for later use in revision.

Idea 6.16

Match the mark scheme

Nearly all examinable subjects have mark schemes and model answers, and these are usually freely available online (log on to the relevant examination board's website and look for 'mark schemes'). This simple task is a great way of getting learners to really understand what the examiners are looking for. Access and print off a minimum of five mark schemes and their associated questions. Either edit out the actual questions from the mark schemes or white these out once printed off. Distribute these to paired learners and ask them to match the associated mark scheme to the questions. A similar activity can be done if you can access model answers. In this case, learners match the model answer to the appropriate mark scheme. Homework can then be set around one particular question.

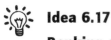 **Idea 6.17**

Ranking statements

This very simple and very effective, well-used idea will create raucous whole-class discussion, so give plenty of warning to your colleagues. Make up 10 contentious statements about your subject area. Print off, laminate and place the statements in envelopes, distributing these to each pair in your class. Each pair then decides on the ranking these statements have in order of agreement/disagreement. Once in agreement, bring pairs together in groups of four. The task now is for each pair to convince the other that their ranking is correct. Once in agreement (and this is where the fun starts) move each group of four into a group of eight, and so on. This activity inevitably ends in a huge whole-classroom discussion and, therefore, requires confident classroom management skills on your part, but it is well worth it!

Questions for professional development

1. How many different seating/table arrangements exist in the institution you teach in? Why are some more effective than others?
2. How many seating strategies have you deployed? Which have been the most successful and why?
3. Have you ever observed a language or drama teacher when they are teaching? If not, why not? The teaching of modern foreign languages and drama contain some of the most advanced active learning strategies and, yet, very few teachers seek or have the opportunity to observe these practitioners in action. Remember that pedagogic strategies associated with one discipline can often be deployed in other areas.

4. Have you ever looked at an educational supplies catalogue? You will be amazed at the range of resources that are available to brighten up any classroom or teaching area. Get friendly with your institution's buying department and spend some time looking at the range of resources available (these are often divided into subject disciplines). Use these to transform the learning space your students walk into and create that 'wow' factor.

Checklist: building your toolbox

- Experiment with different types of music that you have gently playing when learners enter your classroom. Use different genres of music to 'set the scene' at the start of lessons and during task transitions.
- Use smartboards and flip charts, and place the flip chart on the other side of the classroom. This will provide an additional focal point during your teaching and add to the pace and dynamics you are creating in your learning space.
- Ensure that whiteboards, smartboards and flip charts are clean and discard any non-relevant information. Learners coming into your room should only be confronted with information relating to your lesson, and nothing else.
- To reinforce concepts, ensure that key words/concepts/names vital to your lesson are displayed at the start of the lesson so that these can be referred to visually during your teaching and as a source for your questioning strategies.
- Make classroom displays relevant and use them when teaching. Get posters and or/pictures of people related to your subject and refer to them during your lessons (for example, starter activities can be as simple as memorizing the names of five famous people in your displays).

Chapter links

The ideas in this chapter relate closely with those also explored in Chapters 5, 8 and 11.

Further reading

Piaget, J. (1950) *The Psychology of Intelligence*. New York: Routledge.
Wertsch, J.V. (1997) *Vygotsky and the Formation of the Mind*. Cambridge. MA: Harvard University Press.
The above seminal texts have informed and underpinned pedagogic thinking for the past 30 years.

CHAPTER 7

ENGAGING THROUGH E-LEARNING

Chapter overview

The aims of the chapter are to:

1. Provide a simple e-learning toolbox that you can add to, and blend in with, your existing classroom approaches.
2. Offer practical advice on how to structure engaging e-learning ideas into your normal practice and routine.
3. Provide advice and guidance on the use, in particular, of podcasts as a means to stimulate learners.
4. Suggest ways that e-learning can be used to provide support for learners outside normal class time.

Problem-solving

When we talk of e-learning we usually mean 'electronic' or, actually, digitally aided learning. For some, e-learning is best described as *enhanced* learning, or learning supported through the adoption of *emergent* technologies. For Rosenberg (2001) all e-learning has three fundamental characteristics: it is aided through a computer or digital device (mobile or otherwise); it is networked and uses Internet and web-based applications and tools; and it has a broad view of learning. Some commentators also speak of 'M-learning' – using mobile tools and electronic platforms and gadgets, and even of 'blended learning' (Bonk and Graham, 2005) – referring to the mixing of traditional and e-learning strategies.

E-learning certainly is a new and continuing educational 'bandwagon', producing as many uncritical adoptions as it does genuinely exciting and interactive learning opportunities. For some teachers it is the future, and yet for others, it is a scary world of terms and technical know-hows. There is also some belief that learners in the contemporary world are more in tune with e-learning than other means to learn, and we now have the phrase 'digital native' (Prensky, 2001) to describe such thoroughly immersed digital learners, although there is as much critical use of this term as there is evidence for its truth (Bennett et al., 2008).

For many teachers, e-learning appeals as they feel that younger learners are more interested in and stimulated by these approaches. Equally, for others, there is a feeling of powerlessness and helplessness whereby learners know much more than teachers do, and as a consequence the fear is that they might be dismissive of e-learning attempts if they are not 'up to scratch'. E-learning also poses a problem for differentiation: if not all younger learners are 'digital natives' then it might be that e-learning skills are highly polarized, leading to what some call a 'digital divide'. Other teachers have felt that the 'power shift' from the skills of the teacher to the skills and know-how of the learner is the very thing that makes e-learning exciting and an effective motivational tool.

Teachers who have explored e-learning often report that it is time-consuming to set up. Others suggest that while time-consuming in the initial outlay, the motivational benefits – and the quality of the learning itself – far outweigh the effort put in. It is also the case that e-learning – if it is to be used and valued by learners and part of a normal routine – needs heavy 'orchestration' by the teacher, and that teachers adopting e-learning techniques need to be as motivated by them (and demonstrate this to their classes) as they wish their own learners to be.

Context

The Joint Information Systems Committee (JISC) offers evidence that, if used with care and appropriately to match pedagogic need, e-learning strategies can be highly motivating for learners. In the JISC report *In Their Own Words: Exploring the Learners' Perspective on E-learning* (2007) there is a favourable view of e-learning as a means to stimulate and encourage interaction – which itself is seen as motivating and engaging, irrespective of whether emergent technologies are used or not. There is also some evidence available that suggests that learners are increasingly motivated through the use of 'access anytime' and 'consume on the go' mobile learning (through the use of iPods, other media devices such as phones and handhelds and SMS or 'text messaging') (Savill-Smith et al., 2006). Equally, there are many theoretical arguments to suggest that e-learning can have a genuine pedagogic role to play in stimulating communities of learners and in providing tools for interactive learning (Stephenson, 2001).

Many commentators have made cases for the motivational use of social software, whereby learners can build communities online and can interact with one another (JISC, 2007), and podcasts (Salmon et al., 2008), whereby audio recordings are used to provide additional content to learners that can be accessed at any time and downloaded onto portable devices. In this chapter we look at practical ideas for you to add e-learning into your classroom teaching, and to move beyond the classroom with asynchronous (not in 'real time') strategies and techniques.

Toolbox

Using e-learning for the start and end of lessons

As we have noted in Chapters 2 and 5, the start and end of lessons are crucial in setting the tone, capturing learners' attention and connecting learning opportunities together. They are also vital for assessment purposes and for ensuring the right tone. They contribute considerably to building appropriate learning climates. Interactive 'whiteboards' and the availability of a virtual learning environment (VLE) provide a wealth of resources and opportunities to engage and motivate learners at these key moments in a lesson.

 Idea 7.1

Stimulate at the start

Start each lesson – or as many as are appropriate – with a source for learners to consider and then discuss. They could connect the source to prior learning or use the source to guess the aims of the lesson they are about to start. Display or play this resource through the interactive whiteboard in your class. It could be audio, a film or news clip from the Web, a picture or an image. Learners are to discuss what they see/hear and its relevance to what they are studying. This is an effective way to gather everyone's attention at the start of the lesson and, with the presence in your classroom of an interactive whiteboard, you essentially have a networked and Internet-enabled multimedia screen ready to be used.

Idea 7.2

Have a learner scribe

At key moments in group feedback or for plenaries, assign a learner to be the 'scribe' for the class. This could be organized on a rota basis. Ask them to sit at the interactive whiteboard and make notes for the group to summarize the discussion. This frees up the teacher to interact with the group as appropriate. The document can be saved and can be emailed to learners or posted up on a VLE for learners to access and download, providing valuable support materials. This means they do not need to copy down, and are freed up to interact and engage.

 Idea 7.3

Sorting and text boxes

Interactive whiteboards have the ability to display text in 'textboxes' inside Word or other notepad programmes. One of the characteristics of text boxes is that they can be moved around the screen by touching and dragging them; they are not 'locked in place' like normal text. This means the interactive whiteboard can be seen as one giant sorting exercise, with teachers and learners able to move statements, reorder, group and sort – all the traditional tools we often suggest are good for group work and for the start and the end of lessons. Learners could come to the front and have a go as directed by their peers, or teachers could do it as directed by learners. Any activity where learners need to sort and reorder can be done on the screen and, as with Idea 7.2, the outcome can be saved and distributed to learners after the lesson.

 Idea 7.4

Using thumbnails

Most interactive whiteboards have software which enables the use of 'thumbnails' – a screen at the side of the open document which show the pages of the document, or other open documents. This enables the user/viewer to move very easily between documents or pages. On a whiteboard this opens up some excellent possibilities for documents to be compared easily and efficiently by classes. Consider the document produced in Idea 7.2 – a summary produced by learners at the end of a lesson. Over time, you can show classes their previous documents, or even compare between classes, showing them what other learners have thought about the same topic. This is an easy way to reuse the work they produce and to be constantly scaffolding and linking new knowledge to old. It also validates the knowledge and outcomes produced by your class; it shows learning to be worth recording and returning to over time, building a narrative as you go.

Using interactive whiteboards: the whole world in your hands?

When using interactive whiteboards, practitioners have found it useful to consider the following:

- Always regularly 'orientate' the screen and project to maximize efficiency.
- Have your own set of interactive board pen and eraser tools that you carry from class to class – do not rely on the tools being there.
- Carry Blu-Tack as a means to compensate for missing items in the interactive board's equipment tray; Blu-Tack can be placed over the infrared reader, 'tricking' the board into thinking the tools are in place, enabling the board to carry on functioning correctly.
- Use learners as much as possible – get them up out of their seats, touching the board and manipulating text, and so on – make it as interactive for them as it is for you.
- Use the interactive board to show diagrams, pictures, news items, and so on. Really capitalize on the fact that, if connected to the Web, you really do have the 'whole world' at your fingertips. Make the most of this.

Podcasting for learner engagement

A podcast is an audio file that can be played on a website ('streamed') or downloaded for the listener to store and possibly transfer to a mobile device such as a laptop, MP3 player or personal media player (PMP). The term 'podcast' is a conflation of the words 'iPod' and 'broadcast'. Podcasts are the digital files created either by learners or their teachers, and the act of recording a podcast is referred to as 'podcasting'. When podcasting, someone needs to both record the audio and then find a means of 'broadcasting' or making the audio file available for others to find and use. As a simple rule, podcasts contain audio whereas vodcasts contain video. Sometimes we might use the term 'enhanced podcast' to refer to an audio that offers additional information such as hyperlinks to web pages or images to support key sections in the recording. Podcasts can be used as a means to 'lesson capture' learning or teaching sessions, as a means to record 'lectured' additional content or to record feedback to learners. Podcasts need to be 'hosted' somewhere – they need to be uploaded to a webpage or, for many teachers and learners, inside a VLE where they can be found by others.

Reflection point

To record a podcast you need to either have a microphone and recording software or to buy a digital voice recorder that then plugs into the USB port of your computer whereby you can transfer the audio file across, just like any other computer file. Consider what would be best for you and your learners. If you are going to ask your learners to also record their own audio files how will you structure this? What room will you use? Learners presumably could not do this all at the same time, due to the background noise it would generate. Equally, if you work in a busy environment, how, where and at what times will you record your own podcasts? To solve these problems, educational institutions now set aside a space as an e-learning workshop or recording studio.

 Idea 7.5

Record induction messages

Teachers can record messages to learners that can be listened to at the start of the year or course as part of settling in, or as their 'induction'. These audio files can be used by teachers as homework – if they are posted onto the VLE and this can be accessed by learners at a distance, while off site (most can be with appropriate passwords). These messages might explain the year, the topic or might be inspirational in tone – setting the scene and giving advice.

 Idea 7.6

Record homework debriefings

After marking a set of homework – maybe for key homework at specific times of the year – record a podcast offering advice and guidance in general, based upon the marking you have done. This would almost be like an 'examiners' report' but through an audio. Speak through the good and bad points of what you have seen; make suggestions for what learners need to do next. This is an effective way of documenting feedback for learners to return to at a later stage, and a very effective use of teacher time.

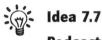

Idea 7.7
Podcast formative assessment feedback

In most VLEs, learners have their own private user areas, which staff can access to upload documents. If this is not the case, it is usually relatively easy for your IT support to configure the VLE you use to provide this feature. Once established, you could make podcasts for individual learners as a means to record formative feedback on their work. As these are individual pieces of feedback, you need to ensure that the files are being uploaded to a private space that only the learner in question can access. There is something extremely intimate, rich and personal about hearing the voice of people you know, and this could make this suggestion extremely supportive and engaging for learners. Each audio would need to be quite small with the key points clearly drawn-out and signposted. It also means that, through tone and inflection in your voice, learners can hear what you really mean; these nuances might be lost with written feedback. It is also probably the case, once you get into the swing, that it would take less time to speak and record feedback than to write extensive comments on someone's work. This suggestion also means that the feedback can be accessed at other times, later in the programme to support learners at different points; it would always be visible as a file in their user area and never likely to be 'lost' or misfiled.

Idea 7.8
Record revision podcasts (1)

Identify key aspects of your curriculum – case studies, important terms, issues – and produce 'bite-sized' podcasts on each. Record small audio files that get right to the point and summarize the issue in question as succinctly as possible. Upload these to the VLE so learners have access to them. Over time you will amass a large collection of support materials for learners to use all through the teaching, and especially at times of revision.

Best practice – think about your podcast pedagogy

When recording podcasts as a means to deliver and convey information, give a thought to how you might structure them; think about what your pedagogy will be. What shape will they have? What pattern will you establish so that learners know what is happening and can follow them easily? Consider the following suggestions:

- Try and record most of your podcasts in roughly the same time – no more than 4–5 minutes. You can always record more than one if you have a large issue to get through.
- 'Chunk' the podcasts into bite-sized bits.
- Have a phrase that you say at the start of every recording where you introduce the aims – just like a lesson; develop this as a common pattern so that over time your listeners are familiar with it.
- Try and do your recording unscripted – do not worry about being slick and smooth – it is you (your learners hear you unscripted all the time)! It will be rich and familiar for them to hear you as naturally as you can be.
- Recap in the middle and again at the end. Remind the listeners what you are doing and what they have heard.
- At the very end tell them how and where they might use the idea/concept/ curriculum knowledge.
- Tell them at the start and/or at the end which other podcasts link to the one they are listening to.

Best practice – take the time to 'code' your podcasts

When recoding podcasts, you have a great deal of options when you get to the point of saving the files and uploading them to be stored on the Web or on a VLE. Really try and explore these options – they make it much easier for learners to find what they are looking for. Consider the following:

- If you are using software (and not a digital voice recorder) take the time to enter as much meta-information about the recording as possible – author, theme, album. All this information will help listeners categorize your podcasts in their music libraries if they import them in this way.
- Think about the titles you give your recordings. Think about the file names – try to identify podcasts that are part of a similar series.
- When uploading each recording to the VLE, enter in some text to explain the key points of the recording. You could use a simple list of key words to do this. This means learners will find what they are looking for more easily.

Idea 7.9
Record revision podcasts (2)

Following on from Idea 7.8, peers could record revision podcasts for each other. They could be given a topic, asked to produce a script for you to check and to then make the recording. This would also encourage them to listen to others, and you might get more learners using your collection of podcasts more quickly.

Idea 7.10
Podcast homework messages and instructions

If learners have a task coming up – maybe for homework, or an extended project over a period of time – you might want to record instructions or advice. This means that learners can listen to what you have to say at the point they need it – and even outside of class time if they are working on the project at home or in the library.

Idea 7.11
Set-up a 'portable podcast station'

Communicate with the library staff what you are doing with your podcasts. See if they would be happy for you to record podcasts and save them onto CDs, so that with headphones and a CD player a portable 'podcast station' could be set up in the library, separate from the computer area. Alternatively, if you invested in a few sets of headphones and players, more than one learner could use the resource at the same time. They could carry it to a desk and work with books, while also using the podcasts. This might simply make them more flexible than being 'tied to a computer desk' to use them.

Reflection point

How do you imagine your learners will consume your podcasts and where will they be at the time? The great thing about podcasts is that they are download-able by the user – providing you set up the appropriate permissions on the VLE

(Continued)

(Continued)

to allow this. This means they can be saved onto a USB Flash stick or saved on the learner's home PC or laptop. Equally, they can be imported by learners into music libraries and, in turn, stored on MP3 devices and some phones. Consider the implications of this. They can be used on the bus, in the library and at home. Talk this through with your learners – get them to see the flexibility these resources offer them.

E-learning for asynchronous support

E-learning is often divided into synchronous and asynchronous activity. By synchronous we mean 'in real time', and conversely, by asynchronous we mean 'not in real time'. For example, a chat room or a video conference is synchronous – learners are in different places connected by the Web, but they are all 'there' at the same time, interacting at the same time. They are 'in the room' together; it is just that the room in question is digital and virtual. On the other hand, posting comments on a blog or forum or downloading a podcast are not in real time. They have the benefit of being accessible by learners at their convenience.

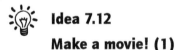 **Idea 7.12**

Make a movie! (1)

Most computers have a movie-making programme pre-installed. These programmes allow the user to manipulate, relatively easily, pictures and video along with overlaying audio as a soundtrack. They then record and save the finished project as a movie file which can then be played back in real time. This feature – often underused and overlooked by many – is an excellent and assessable way for teachers and learners to make simple but effect movies. This could be an excellent group project (rather than a presentation?) or an interesting homework, providing enough time and support is in place to ensure all learners have fair access to the necessary equipment. These movie files can be posted on the VLE and accessed outside of the school/college day.

Idea 7.13
Make a movie! (2)

Teachers could use the movie-making suggestion discussed in Idea 7.12 to record an introduction to the new classes or new topics. These movies could be sent to learners via email or a learner could be asked to log on and view the movie at a specific time. This could be a really exciting and unusual way to 'whet their appetite' before coming to see you for the first time, and to really raise expectations.

Idea 7.14
Surgery blog

At times of revision before examinations and tests – or at other key points in the year – you could set up a blog or forum whereby learners and you (and your colleagues) can interact outside of lessons and support each other. This might be especially effective if you teach older learners who have study leave. Most VLEs have the ability to host 'discussion groups' or for learners to post comments on 'threads' which you can set up. Sometimes these features are called different things, and sometimes you might need to ask IT support staff to enable the feature for you if it does not come as standard. This would mean that you can set up a virtual 'surgery' whereby learners can get help from each other and from you. This would be asynchronous support – it is not a 'chat room' – it does not exist in real time, but users post comments as they wish.

 Reflection point

E-safety is of huge importance for safeguarding young learners in virtual and digital environments. Think about how you will do this and what your institution's policies and rules are about it. As a teacher in a digital world you have both a moral and legal responsibility to e-moderate and spot e-bullying. If you are asking learners to participate in chat, forums or blogs you need to set the rules, and everyone needs to be clear on them. For future guidance you might like to refer to the 2008 Byron Review, *Safer Children in a Digital World* (DCSF, 2008), available for download for free from the DCSF.

Idea 7.15

SMS homework messages

With the appropriate permission of your institution – and the volunteering of your learners – mobile phone text messaging (or, SMS) can be used to inform learners of deadlines, updates to your VLE resources and, even, provide text describing homework tasks. To provide this service you will need to talk openly to your institution and your learners about the implications involved in having learners' mobile phone numbers and also to decide from which phone the messages will be sent.

Idea 7.16

Tweet homework

Micro-blogging sites are very popular today, as are other social media such as Facebook. Micro-blogging means to update your 'followers' or 'friends' with small messages – often limited to 140–150 characters – the same size as text messages a few years ago, before the rise of third-generation multimedia mobile phones. Twitter is a good example of a micro-blogging site, but there are many others. This could be an effective way to distribute messages and homework tasks. As with all digital safety, you would need permission from your institution to enter an online space with your learners that is not held within your actual VLE. Having said this, most VLEs offer a message service which would produce similar results.

Idea 7.17

Tweet reading suggestions

Following on from the suggestion to use micro-blogging tools (see Idea 7.16), the same idea would apply to reading and online sources and resources. You could micro-blog hyperlinks to sites that you know would aid learners in their revision, projects and coursework.

Questions for professional development

1. Have you recorded podcasts? How have the learners responded to them? How have you encouraged them to access them?

2. If you have success with using e-learning tools such as podcasts and movie-making, try to disseminate the lessons learned to your colleagues.
3. What e-learning tools have you used that take the least time to set up but have the greatest impact in terms of learner use and engagement? Why is this?
4. Which aspects of e-learning do you need further support on?

Checklist: building your toolbox

- Consider how you can use your VLE as a means to house podcasts and videos that can be accessed and downloaded outside of class time.
- Record a bank of podcasts as a means to provide extra support for your learners – they are reusable every year and will build up into an excellent resource. You could also encourage all staff and colleagues in your team to participate in a podcasting curriculum development project.
- You might wish to consider podcasts for formative assessment.
- Liaise with the library and other colleagues to ensure that podcasts are as accessible to all as possible.
- Speak to your learners about what they would like – get them to make suggestions and recommendations for online materials.
- Use the interactive board as an excellent means to record the outcomes of plenaries – and to be able to save and distribute these at a later stage.
- Investigate the degree to which your learners would use phones, SMS, media players and other such devices for M-learning.

Chapter links

The ideas in this chapter relate closely with those explored in Chapters 6, 9, 10 and 13.

Further reading

Richardson, W. (2010) *Blogs, Wikis, Podcasts and Other Powerful Web Tools for Classrooms*, 3rd edn. Thousand Oaks, CA: Corwin.
This text, although primarily for the US market, offers some really useful advice on using podcasts, wikis and blogs. There are some excellent suggestions here written in a very accessible way.

Kidd, W. and Czerniawski, G. (2010) *Successful Teaching 14–19: Theory, practice and reflection*. London: Sage.
In this, our other book, we consider, in a discrete chapter, how you can adopt e-learning and blended learning approaches to enhance learning inside and outside your classroom.

CHAPTER 8

CLASSROOM MANAGEMENT AND LEARNER ENGAGEMENT

Chapter overview

The aims of the chapter are to:

1. Illustrate the connections between motivation, engagement and desirable behaviour.
2. Explore techniques that enable first lessons to 'start as you mean to go on'.
3. Illustrate ways in which teachers can settle learners down at the start of a lesson.
4. Provide strategies for getting and keeping learners 'on task'.

Problem-solving

Classroom management is one of those aspects of classroom teaching that many new and experienced teachers find time-consuming and at times difficult. This is especially true for new teachers and for those coming into contact with new groups they have not taught before; this could apply to classes taken over from colleagues, new learners arriving at your institution for the first time, or lessons right at the start of the year. We feel that good learner–teacher relationships are the key to productive learning and to classroom management and ethos. We also believe that the climate you establish with your class directly affects the amount and type of classroom disruption you might get. Therefore, we come to the conclusion that investing time in classroom management and classroom climate-building activities is a really productive aspect of professional practice. It is not something to ignore, thinking 'I want to get on with the teaching', because good management and climate are *essential building-blocks* in teaching – and they are essential preconditions for effective learning and exciting and creative classes.

We favour the term 'classroom management' rather than the perhaps more pejorative 'behaviour management'. We feel that it is more helpful to see teachers as managing the whole of the learning process – the resources, support, behaviour, opportunities, climate, and challenge.

The ideas in this chapter cover issues of clear and effective instruction and communication, ways to start lessons and keep learners on track and on task, ideas for building and maintaining a positive learning atmosphere, and some principles for dealing with disruption. As you can see, classroom management is much wider than simply managing behaviour – although it encompasses this too. As represented in Figure 8.1, we believe that positive learning relationships with high expectations of learners are the essential requirements of both a motivated classroom and a well-managed and well-behaved classroom. These

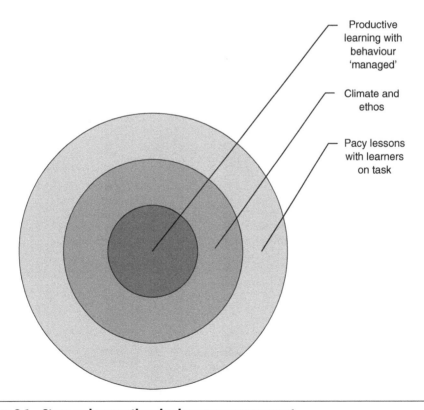

Productive
learning with
behaviour
'managed'

Climate and
ethos

Pacy lessons
with learners
on task

Figure 8.1   Steps and connections in classroom management

positive relationships are at the heart of our practice, with good, pacy, stimulating teaching at the heart of what we do, leading to good classroom management.

Context

Gilbert (2002) says that 'motivation is a four letter word' and that word is 'hope'. By this, Gilbert means that encouraging learners to believe that they can learn and that their learning will be productive is one of the keys to learners' success. It is also an often overlooked key. For our purposes here, we suggest that classroom management is also a 'four letter word' – hope. If you are able to be positive about your learners, their potential and abilities, and instil in them the same positive regard for their own learning (and to respect and value your support of them), then we feel that you will have less 'disruption' to deal with. Perhaps the key to 'behaviour management' is actually how you frame and communicate your expectations of your learners and your own professional persona?

It might seem strange discussing issues of behaviour and classroom management in a book on motivation. Yet, we believe the key to motivation is that learners feel engaged and learning is seen as worthwhile. We also believe that the key to learners displaying appropriate behaviours is their engagement with their learning. Thus, as represented in Figure 8.2, pace, climate, motivation, engagement, behaviour and teacher management are all interlinked and are symbiotic – they are interdependent and affect each other.

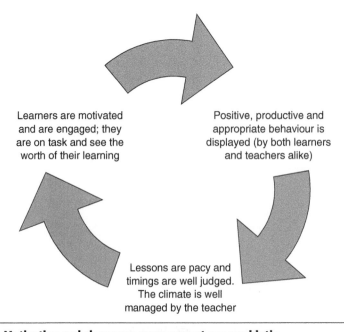

Learners are motivated and are engaged; they are on task and see the worth of their learning

Positive, productive and appropriate behaviour is displayed (by both learners and teachers alike)

Lessons are pacy and timings are well judged. The climate is well managed by the teacher

Figure 8.2   Motivation and classroom management are symbiotic

Toolbox

Start as you mean to go on . . .

Those first few lessons with a new group are really key to establishing both the 'rules' of the group and the climate of the learning environment. This is something we also discuss in Chapters 1 and 2. Those first few lessons are an opportunity for you to 'show your professional self' – to establish with the group what you expect, what they should expect and also to validate what sort of teacher you are. This is key: you need to have learners leaving your first few lessons clearly understanding what being with you and being supported and taught by you will be like. While trite to say, it is true that first impressions do count.

 Idea 8.1

Meet and greet

This is something very simple but works really well, ideal for the first time when meeting a group, but something we recommend you continue all through your teaching year. Meet all the learners at the door of the classroom and greet them. Say hello, welcome them into the room, direct them to their seats or at least try and make eye contact and tell them to 'put bags away' or 'get folders out', and so on. Do this as pleasantly as possible. It is very difficult to be disruptive or confrontational to someone who has asked you how you are and greeted you. You would be surprised how effective this is in establishing both rapport and a good climate. Many teachers are in the corner of the room, or have their backs to learners, effectively ignoring them. Make sure everyone has been contacted. There is nothing worse than learners going through their day without teachers talking, chatting and greeting them.

 Idea 8.2

Manage your professional self

Think about how you are going to communicate to your learners, at the start of those first few lessons, what sort of teacher you are. So many teachers ignore this. Many start first lessons with a discussion of 'rules' and 'expectations' (which are all valuable), but in doing so they ignore the fact that teaching is social and

(Continued)

(Continued)

relational – based upon getting to know a group and the group getting to know you. At the start of your relationship with a new group, take the time to explain to them what your teaching is like. Tell them exactly what you will be doing in the classroom, and why. Tell them what you believe about learning and how it works. Sell your pedagogy to them in a way that they will understand.

 Reflection point

Think about what your expectations are of your learners. And now think about what sort of teacher you believe you are. What do you value? Why do you teach how you do? Why do you think it is right and productive to teach in this way? How do you know? In thinking about these issues you can better understand what it is you need to communicate to your learners about yourself and the time that they spend with you. Find an opportunity to have this discussion with learners at the start of your relationship with them.

 Idea 8.3

Set the rules (part 1)

One way of establishing rules with a new class is to ask them to write the rules themselves. Ask them, in groups or pairs, to write out how they would want to be treated – both by their other classmates and by yourself. Get the group to agree on the common and important rules and then post them up on your walls. It gives you something to go back to at moments of disruption – you can explain that 'we all set the rules together'.

 Idea 8.4

Set the rules (part 2)

Often, as teachers, we need to find pedagogic and classroom management techniques and strategies that suit us – our personalities, professional personas and what we feel comfortable with. There are, therefore, many different ways to achieve the same result. As a compete contrast to the suggestion in Idea 8.3, you could try the opposite: not setting the rules at all! We do not mean telling learners the rules rather than getting the learners to tell you. Rather, we mean simply being very clear you are not going to tell them the rules! You could explain to them that you know they know the rules – and so you are not going to go through them. You know they know how to behave and that you have the same expectations as all their other teachers. This works surprisingly well with older learners.

Idea 8.5
Idle chit-chat

Make an effect to speak to learners in corridors, libraries, the lunch queue, and so on. Make an effort to be personable rather than rushing down corridors from room to room. Difficult, granted, depending upon the layout of your institution and the layout of your timetable. However, it really helps for your presence to be 'known' to the community you work in and with.

Idea 8.6
The honesty box

You could try this within the first few weeks with a new group. Get a box or container and ask learners to put into the box on slips of paper – written confidentially – things they do and do not like; things they think are working well; aspects of the curriculum they feel need to be returned to. Try and explore with them the pedagogic choices and techniques they think suit them and those that they feel do not. Once you have your contributions – perhaps done as they exit at the end of a lesson – you need to be seen to return to them at a later stage and follow them up. Perhaps a 'group meeting' or an explanation from yourself as to why you are doing what you are doing. Make the learners feel involved in the process – make them truly see themselves as entering into a partnership with you and as a stakeholder in their own learning. This does wonders for the classroom climate and for your relationship with them, if managed correctly.

Idea 8.7

Believe in it yourself

Always assume that learners will be well behaved and that they will meet deadlines on time. Tell them that you know everyone will meet all the deadlines and will do all their homework. Try and give the impression that what you expect is both normal and appropriate. Believe and communicate this belief and you might be surprised what happens. Teachers who always get homework in and always have well-managed lessons often start from the position that this is normal and expected.

Settling learners in

The start of a lesson is well recognized as a moment of potential disruption and chaos. This is due, largely, to the many different variables you need to manage: you need to get your class into the room, seated (and this may vary from lesson to lesson), silent enough for the start of the lesson, and you need to explain the session and its aims and objectives. If you get this right, and can launch into productive learning as quickly as possible, then often the climate and momentum of the lesson (its 'pace') runs on a course of its own and learners are caught up in the tempo, unable to derail or get distracted. This means that starters need to be as meaningful as possible and also need to capture everyone's attention.

Idea 8.8

Start with assessment of prior learning

Many successful teachers start with an assessment of prior learning. This can be undertaken in a variety of different ways. For example, you might consider:

- Group activities such as sorting or grouping activities.
- Making mindmaps and overviews/summaries.
- Learners can make lists of the key points they can remember to date.
- Learners can complete simple quizzes or tests.
- Questions can be asked from 'flash cards'.

The assessment of prior learning can take the form of individual work in silence, group work or can be whole class. It is a comfortable and pedagogically useful way to settle learners in and also to motivate them.

Idea 8.9
Start with a task

An effective way to settle learners down is to start straight away with a task. Sometimes this might even be done before the aims and objectives of the session – as long as learners are clear about this and the task itself fits in, in some way. The task means learners can be as productive as possible as quickly as possible. It also means that individuals can be directly managed as the rest of the class works.

Idea 8.10
Aim to do more. . .

Many teachers recognize the need, partly due to national strategies and how these affect institutional policies, to address aims and objectives at the start of the lesson. You could go further, however, and really try and communicate the point behind what the learners will be doing. Most teachers start with a version of 'the aims are. . ..', some go further and then explain 'firstly we will be doing XXX, and secondly XXX and so on', but many do not then go further still and explain 'and the reason why you are doing this today is XXX'. Do not assume that your learners do see the point; explain to them what the point is. This often increases engagement but also decreases disruption as learners value the worth of the exercises and tasks, once they understand them fully.

Idea 8.11
Use homework

If learners are bringing homework into the session – or getting marked homework back – this is an excellent opportunity to draw them in quickly, right at the start. You could do this directly before the aims of the session or directly afterwards. Use the homework for peer marking, highlighting and annotating, identifying key words, making summaries or to help complete group extension tasks. It is an effective way to ensure homework is done (because it is seen by learners to then have a point) and also to get learners active and involved.

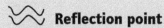 **Reflection point**

Starts of lessons (due to their importance and also 'discrete' nature) are excellent opportunities for collaborative observational practice between colleagues. You could observe other teachers and how they settle learners down or as part of wider CPD draw up within your teams (or across your institution as a whole) a list of strategies that you and colleagues have found productive. Try to vary what you do to maintain interest but at the same time be aware (and reflect upon) what does work, and in particular what captures learners the quickest. Vary your routine but also find and establish a pattern that works for you and your learners. Do not be afraid to experiment.

 Idea 8.12

Make an entrance

You might wish to explore the notion of playing 'entrance music' for your class as they come in and settle down. What often happens in these circumstances is that switching off the music signifies the start of the session and the class goes silent – expecting you to start. You can move to the centre front of the room and everyone stops as they know what is about to happen. It is almost as if the curtain has been raised on a stage.

Best practice – effective starters

Practitioners have found the following starting techniques and strategies highly effective in making as productive and pacy a start as possible:

- Using a case study or picture/text as a means to open up creative discussions as to what the lesson will be on – to provoke thought and stimulate interest.
- Assess prior learning as a means to settle everyone into an activity as quickly as possible.
- Playing music as a 'cue' to demarking when the lesson starts.
- Using peer assessment – often linked to going through and annotating homework.
- Silent mindmapping exercises.

Idea 8.13
Pace and flow

Planning a variety of tasks with enough time for plenaries and recaps in between them is a really useful means to ensure that learners can be on task for as much as possible – with lots of opportunities for feedback and discussion before moving on to the next task. This considerably reduces low-level disruption. Scaffolding tasks so that each one leads to the next is also a means to ensure the session flows and that the tempo or momentum carries learners along with it.

Reflection point

Be sensitive to how the pace and flow of the lesson is going. Especially if learners and groups have been doing one task for some time. If the noise starts to rise or you feel many are off task, start to make decisions regarding whether or not you continue the activity. You could step in and support. You could regroup and get feedback before allowing learners to continue on again.

Keeping learners on task

Once learners are settled and the lesson has started, the next step is to keep them engaged. We say, keeping them 'on task'; in other words, keeping them involved in their learning and the learning being as productive as possible. Some of this is about how you communicate instruction and some of this is about the task itself being worthwhile and appropriately challenging. However, a great deal of this is about the strategies you can adopt to keep everyone on task – and knowing when to intervene, and when not to.

Best practice – effective communication techniques

Practitioners have found it effective to ensure that communication with learners is always clear. This minimizes disruption due to the lack of clarity of the communication itself. Consider the following principles of effective communication:

- Do not ask unnecessary questions.
- If you are about to give an instruction, then make everyone aware that you are asking them to do something and tell them when they are to do it.

(Continued)

(Continued)

- Do not set learners off on a task and then disrupt them with further instructions you might have originally forgotten.
- Do not ask 'will you' if you mean 'now do'; do not pose it as a choice or option when it is not.
- When asking someone to take part when they are not, focus on the desired behaviour rather than the undesired one. Do not say 'Can you stop doing XXX', but instead say 'What we are all doing now is XXX'. Reinforce the outcome you want rather than draw attention to the misbehaviour.
- Do not start an instruction and then interrupt your own half-spoken sentence by changing your mind with a different instruction. Be clear before you speak.
- Preface discipline with something positive if you can – this is especially effective when speaking to learners as individuals. Start by saying, 'It's good that XXX . . . but remember that XXX'. Always make it clear what the desired and appropriate outcome is.

Idea 8.14

Go walkabout

Ensure you are moving around between learners and groups. Make sure every part of the room is accessible to you and that you are not stuck in a corner or at the front. Walk around and kneel alongside learners or crouch down to chat to them. Try not to tower above or be removed at the front, at a distance.

Idea 8.15

Do not disrupt the disruptors

Once learners are settled and working, do not then disrupt them with unnecessary instruction or elaboration. If someone who has been off task is back on task again, try to leave them to it as much as you can, rather than reinforcing the undesired behaviour and causing them to be off task all over again. The point is not that they behave. The point is that they learn – and they behave in order to learn as effectively as possible. Do not get sidetracked into thinking the point is their behaviour and that appropriate behaviour is a measure of the lesson's success. It is a precursor to what is important – learning.

Idea 8.16

Offer support not discipline

It is highly motivating for learners to be offered support and help. This is often why some individuals do end up disrupting – they need help. Offer as much support and outside of class help as you spend time on discipline. Make sure the relationship with each individual has the balance right: their learning is what should take up the majority of their time with you; not you disciplining them.

Idea 8.17

Use cueing

Alongside what we do and do not say and choose to say, we also communicate in other ways: non-verbally through signs and gestures. These are as important to effective communication as our words and tones. Consider the following:

- Clapping at the start of a lesson to signify the start.
- Raising your hands in the air to get the attention of a large group.
- Using a blocking motion with your palm to stop low level disruption.
- Making a 'dampening' gesture with both hands lowering palms down to illustrate the need for a group to soften and reduce noise.
- Traffic-directing question and answer, where you block one interruption with one hand and allow another to continue with the other.
- Waving at individuals who are off task.

A great many of these – in the right context, of course – can be applied without any words at all. Thus, you continue in what you are doing, using the non-verbal cueing without allowing potential disruption to actually disrupt.

 Reflection point

Spend a moment thinking about the non-verbal gestures you make in the classroom. What about other teachers when you see them teach? Are there cues you can take and incorporate into your own practice? Using body language as a technique is as much part of your pedagogic repertoire as any other teaching technique, but as they seem personal we often do not consider them. Yet we use them all the time.

Best practice – effective classroom management techniques

Practitioners have found the following principles of effective classroom management useful in helping them deal with disruption and other moments which might potentially derail a lesson:

- Never have public confrontations.
- Never get angry – always maintain your professional persona.
- If you do discipline a learner, try to be quick to follow this up with support or a 'normal' classroom interaction so that the act of discipline does not define the interaction or their (and your) experience of the lesson.
- Follow up significant incidents afterwards in private.
- Do not take on battles you cannot win.
- Try 'tactical ignoring' – it is much healthier for the learning climate to not have a teacher constantly and repeatedly disciplining; only discipline when it counts.
- Use non-confrontational hand signals to stop, block and limit chat and disruption.
- Do not point and do not invade learners' own personal space.
- Try to communicate 'on a level' with learners, making eye contact if you are asking them to do something.
- Keep statements for discipline as brief as possible – do not go on or make your intervention longer than the disruption itself.
- Reward desired behaviour.
- Thank learners for stopping confrontation or disruption when they do.
- Absolutely avoid sarcasm.
- Do not ask questions or give instructions you do not mean. Do not *ask* them to obey the rules when you do not mean this. Simply instruct purposefully, quickly and communicate what you mean as well as you can.
- Be as even-handed and as consistent as you can be in applying your rules and expectations.

Questions for professional development

1. Think about how you will communicate your expectations to your learners. Have you tried to do this, based upon the ideas in this chapter? How did it work? Were learners surprised you were doing this and did you feel they appreciated it?
2. Have you explored with colleagues different ideas for starters that settle learners down easily and effectively? This might be a very useful exchange to have in meetings, on training days or as part of wider CPD contributions.

3. What non-verbal cueing do you use that is most effective?
4. Think about how you are able to manage the room by moving around it. Do you need to lay out your room differently (see Chapter 6) to ensure you have access to all areas and groups?

Checklist: building your toolbox

- Greet learners at the door.
- Establish your professional presence by being supportive and communicative in corridors, libraries and other such spaces.
- Explore playing music as a means to signify the start of a lesson.
- Plan for pace and variety.
- Have a task ready right at the start of the session to settle learners down.
- Be very conscious (and reflect upon and practise) your communication.
- Equally, be conscious about the non-verbal cues you use. Develop cues that you can see work.
- Think about how you will set rules and expectations.

Chapter links

The ideas in this chapter relate closely with those also explored in Chapters 1, 2, 4 and 5.

Further reading

Gilbert, I. (2002) *Essential Motivation in the Classroom*. London: Routledge/Falmer.
This excellent bite-sized book applies a range of motivational theories to teaching, learning and thinking in the classroom.

Rogers, B. (1998) *You Know the Fair Rule: Strategies for Making the Hard Job of Discipline and Behaviour Management in School Easier,* 2nd edn. London: Prentice Hall.
This book provides a wide range of practical advice and techniques for classroom interaction and avoiding confrontation.

Rogers, B. (2011) *Classroom Behaviour: A Practical Guide to Effective Teaching, Behaviour Management and Colleague Support*, 3rd edn. London: Sage.
This book provides a very interesting repertoire of classroom management tools for the practitioner.

CHAPTER 9

FEEDBACK AND FEEDFORWARD

Chapter overview

The aims of the chapter are to:

1. Suggest strategies for teachers to formatively, summatively and ipsatively record their assessment decisions.
2. Offer ideas that include learners in the evaluation of their own progress.
3. Suggest advice and guidance to teachers on how to reduce their overall marking workloads.
4. Embed categories into teachers' mark books/records to enable best practice in assessment.

Problem-solving

In Chapter 3 we introduced you to a number of strategies emphasizing that regular formative assessment is incredibly powerful in raising standards. In this sense 'feedback' is better thought of as 'feedforward', that is, the best feedback to learners is that which indicates to them how they can improve in the future. This simple acknowledgement has huge implications for the nature and purpose of record-keeping, assessment practices, monitoring, and the quality and timing of advice that you give to your learners, the professionals working with them and other important stakeholders (for example, parents, social workers). Recent advances in technology mean that the quality and quantity of data that schools and colleges generate, store and re-create is extremely sophisticated. However, all too often, such data is narrowly focused on the 'academic' rather than any holistic view of the learner. In this chapter we offer ideas about record-keeping, monitoring, advice and guidance, embracing the summative, ipsative and formative forms of assessment that we looked at in Chapter 3.

Context

Once qualified, most teachers in schools and colleges constantly attend a succession of parents' evenings, open days/evenings, departmental meetings, and so on where students will be the topic of conversation between educational stakeholders interested in the information you have gleaned from working with them. Those of you working in schools will, within the first few weeks of any term, attend parents' evenings where upwards of 180 parents might expect you to answer questions about their much loved offspring's progress, strengths, weaknesses, and so on. Whether you keep this information in your laptop, personal organizer, PC, or even an old-fashioned 'mark book', the nature and purpose of the records you keep will speak volumes about your overall philosophy of education and will make up an essential part of your teacher's toolbox. Such records can be used to inform not only your learner's progress, but also the success of your own teaching strategies. They can be invaluable for those 30-second corridor conversations with other members of staff and, in some cases, your records will save lives. This last point raises the issue of assessment as a tool in identifying educational performance (or its sudden downturn) as indicative of other graver or more sinister personal issues/circumstances that teachers have to be legally and morally aware of.

Toolbox

Possible data for record-keeping

Assessment without adequate feedback, at best, leaves learners in the dark about their learning and, at worst, demotivates and alienates learners. Get this information right and your 'feedforward' will inform learning experiences that can transform the lives of your teenage learners and provide you with valuable information to improve your own teaching strategies. This is the spirit behind Assessment for Learning (see Chapter 3). Creating the right types of categories in your assessment records (even if you do not always refer to them) will also sensitize you to any potential dangers that some learners might be experiencing in their private lives (for example, sexual abuse, violence, eating disorders). Ideas 9.1 to 9.5 offer you suggestions for the types of categories you might like to create in your assessment records and can be adapted to fit the nature and the purpose of the institution in which you teach.

Idea 9.1
Who's who?

Life will become easier if you know exactly who is who in the lives of your learners. Your records can therefore include: name/gender/age and ethnicity of your students and whether or not they have siblings in your institution. Records can include the contact names/emails of any outside agencies (for example social workers; probation officers); names of teaching assistants/SENCO; heads of year/form tutors; learning mentors; and, finally, parental/guardian contact details (but do not forget to get the mobile telephone numbers of not only parents/guardians but also of your learners).

Idea 9.2
Their past life

All too often we know far too little about our learners even though much information is almost certainly kept on record somewhere – perhaps at their previous school/college. You should therefore attempt to find out and store the following information, if appropriate: medical history (for example, dyslexia; dyspraxia; eyesight; hearing); whether they have been registered as SEN/EAL/G&T; whether they have had any work experience; their overall academic performance; relationships with others; time spent abroad; formal tests/public examinations.

Idea 9.3
Their present life

Teachers are busy people and very often have little time to engage with students about what they do outside the classroom. And yet any interest you show will (even if it is not publicly acknowledged by the student) show them you care and provides you with a bigger picture about what they are capable of doing. Categories in your mark book can include their hobbies; sports; part-time work; awards; after-school activities; languages spoken; UCAS statements; personal statements; local community work; youth clubs attended; and courses (for example, Duke of Edinburgh Award).

Idea 9.4

Academic performance

In terms of how students perform academically, there are a variety of indicators you can weave into your assessment records. These include: a 'hands up' column; target/assessment levels; Key Stage 2/3 cognitive ability test/standard assessment task (CAT/SAT) scores; communication skills; numeracy/literacy/mathematics; end of topic tests; homework grades; credits/merits/prizes; behaviour; responses to questioning; sanctions imposed; detentions; referrals; Diploma Pathway; predicted grades; reading age/spelling age; traffic lights; functional skills; Personal Thinking and Learning Skills (PTLS); contributions in lessons; examination candidate number; coursework dates; folder check/exercise-book check; targets set; learners designated a learning support assistant (LSA); effort/motivation.

Idea 9.5

Well-being

Teachers need to be on the constant lookout for any signs that their teenage learners are becoming disengaged from learning. Sometimes this can be purely a matter of boredom with school/college life, but disengagement can also be a symptom of graver issues to do with well-being and child safety. Both require teachers to be become sensitized to any variation in patterns of behaviour, performance, mood, and so on. Any changes in the categories already mentioned could be telltale signs of trouble at home/on the street, and so on. Depending on whether you work in a school or college, include the following categories: uniform/sports kit; attendance; lateness; mood; personality; organization skills; interpersonal skills; intrapersonal skills.

Reflection point

Your ability to maintain consistently excellent teaching and assessment of learning will, in part, depend on the strategies you develop to deal with the high volume of marking that is an inevitable aspect of being a full-time teacher. It is therefore important that you reflect on your own organizational skills when marking work. One strategy that some teachers adopt is to colour-code batches of folders/exercise books in any one class. For example, put a red sticker on a quarter of the books, a green sticker on the next quarter, and so on. This means that you can then call in those learners' work with red stickers one week, a green sticker the next and so on, and spread the mark load while ensuring that everything is covered.

 Reflection point

As teachers, we possess an 'ethics of care' that embraces both the academic and the pastoral sides of teaching. By carefully constructing your assessment records you will be able to 'sensitize' yourself to any telltale signs related to the welfare of that young person and, if necessary, alert other professionals you work with about any concerns you may have. In this way you will have evidence to back up any fears you might have. Sharing this information with other colleagues could, in some cases, make all the difference in the world to that young person and highlight how important your own ethics of care are to your professional role as a teacher.

Giving written feedback/feedforward

If you did not possess good organizational skills before you went into teaching, then you surely will once you are firmly embedded in the profession. The marking of students' work will, undoubtedly, represent one of the biggest aspects of your teaching workload, so ensure that you make marking as easy as possible – have a procedure and stick to it. Get out that diary and stagger when you set homework for different classes, marking each batch of work the moment it comes in. Be selective about what you mark, when and why, and do not mark unnecessarily. Timetable your marking and choose a time of day and location where there are no distractions (remember that types of marking vary as do suitable locations, for example, many teachers mark tests on train/bus journeys). Time spent on work should be appropriate to the work done, so remember that the first three or four pieces of work you mark will always take longer than the rest. Make sure that you choose three or four students across the ability range to mark first so that you get a good overall sense of what the standard of work will be. Do not mark out every single mistake but, rather, focus on specific issues related to any generic targets you will be setting for the class at the end of the assessed piece of work. We hope that some of the following advice and guidance will help you in giving quality feedback while ensuring that you still have the energy and patience essential for good teaching.

 Reflection point

Do you know who are the learning/teaching assistants within the institution you work? Can you establish strong working relationships with them whereby they work closely with your students based on your targeted feedback? In this way it is then possible for your learners to go directly to them and work on your assessment feedback. This will make your marking individualized and meaningful to them, and allow them to work specifically on areas of weakness that you have identified.

 Idea 9.6

Dialogue marking

Human interaction in assessment practices is essential. Devise a set of codes (for example, Sp = spelling; C = concept) and write these codes as a form of feedback to your learners. Learners must examine their written work and correctly identify what the codes mean and verbally feedback to you their corrections in light of the codes you have written (for example, how to spell the word; their correct interpretation of the concept). Individual tasks can always be set in the written feedback and time allocated in any lesson for the work to be reviewed and comments to be followed up (for example, 'Ask your partner to explain X to you . . .'; 'Go to page 57 and read and then explain this to . . .').

Idea 9.7

Develop a key/code system

Develop a system of codes in both your mark book and the feedback you give your students. Code your target-setting so that students know exactly which areas they must improve on (for example, 'P' = presentation; 'D' = more detail; 'E' = evidence; 'K' = key concepts; 'SPAG' = spelling and grammar). Using your records, you can then ensure that any targets set build on those that you have set previously, rather than simply setting the same targets again and again to the same student. Many teachers use 'WWW' ('What Went Well') and 'EBI' ('Even Better If') in their feedback. Traffic lights (see Chapter 3): green for excellent, amber for satisfactory/partially understood and red for unsatisfactory/not understood can be used in a variety of ways as codes for you to record how well students are doing.

Idea 9.8

To grade or not to grade?

Institutional policies vary but, in general, if marking provides a grade and an annotation, learners are more likely to pay attention to one and not the other, that is, either the grade or the annotation, so choose carefully which technique you will use, vary this but be consistent in how/when you vary making sure that you deploy both strategies over a period of time. Providing the particular student is happy with this, photocopy any graded work that is very good and either display it on the wall or give it back to students to model the good practice of exemplary work carried out by their peers. When annotating, focus on how the student can improve their work to the next level. Remember to set SMART targets (see Chapter 3) on any written feedback, while ensuring that the learner is capable of carrying out the target you set.

Idea 9.9

Red pen, green pen, crosses and ticks

While practice and academia vary enormously on the merits of how feedback should be written, try to avoid the use of red pen when commenting on students' work. Many English as an additional language (EAL) and special educational needs (SEN) students associate the colour red with being wrong and its use can demotivate many learners. Many excellent teachers consequently use green pen when marking work. Avoid crosses for the same reasons, and underline weaknesses, adding comments where necessary on how the learner can improve. By all means tick, but ensure that you do not just tick for the sake of it – underline the work/sentence that the tick refers to so that the learner can quickly visually identify what it is they are doing well.

Best practice – online testing

Many subjects use online testing as a way to set homework which requires little or no marking on the part of the teacher. While we do not advocate 'little or no marking', a range of assessment strategies is vital and can ease the workload of both teacher and student if carefully managed. Increasingly, in many institutions, students are issued with a password and will then sit a vocabulary/concept test based on the work that they have covered with the teacher. Learners who do not reach the required pass mark must re-sit the test at the end of the school/college day. Providing the website is appropriate, students tend to revise and pass, not wishing to re-sit the test at the end of the day. Increasingly most website-based tests are fun and students enjoy this form of assessment.

 ## Reflection point

Black and Wiliam (1998) argue that learning and motivation for learning can be increased through the adoption of a 'medal and mission' approach to assessment and feedback. The 'medal' shows what is positive about the work (that is, the 'reward') and the 'mission' sets targets for future learning (that is, the next steps). Although the 'medal and mission' approach is currently linked to notions of learner ownership of their own learning, previously this approach has been more closely associated with behaviourist techniques of reward and reinforcement. How do you think the use of rewards might motivate learners? Do you agree with this approach?

 ## Idea 9.10

Parents and guardians – the good times and the bad

All too often parents/guardians receive phone calls/emails/letters about what their daughter/son has not done/achieved/passed and, sadly, all too often we,

(Continued)

(Continued)

the teaching profession, fail to make phone calls to those who are closest to our learners that praise rather than admonish. When marking work, ensure that you make a couple of calls home that praise – this does not necessarily have to be for the best work – it can also be for work that shows huge improvement. Design/buy postcards that can be sent home that reward/praise work done in class. Of course, it is also essential that you quickly follow up work not done or work that rapidly shows deterioration, but the impact that positive parental contact has on educational achievement is undervalued by many teachers and hugely valued by parents and learners if/when it takes place.

Including learners in the evaluation of their own work

The role played by peer support and peer learning is central to ipsative assessment, offering an invaluable array of strategies for you to consider when working with your learners. Ipsative assessment refers to a process of self-assessment where the learner identifies his or her own position within his or her learning and assesses his or her own needs. This can be done in isolation or working with other students. The following strategies offer ways for learners to assess each other, freeing you up to monitor more effectively and efficiently the progress of each individual learner.

Best practice – maximizing effectiveness in class

By now you will realize that as teachers/authors we never advocate sitting behind desks when your learners are with you. Timed written work will, it is true, allow you an opportunity to mark work but will also provide even more work for you to assess unless you deploy some of the peer-assessment strategies we introduce to you later in this chapter. However there is much that you can do in class that can ease the marking workload that many teachers experience. The following tips have been gleaned from colleagues we have observed over many years:

- Give pupils sufficient time to read what you have written in your feedback about their work and highlight any advice that they can carry forward into future practice.
- Get students to set three targets in response to your feedback that they must write down (in homework diaries and at the start of their next homework). In

addition to the next work you mark, you can assess to what extent they have met their own targets.

- Get parents/guardians to read and sign the targets at the start of any home-work so that they have a sense of how your student feels about progress made. Follow up with a discussion about the targets either via a quick phone call or a chat at the parents' evening to ensure that they are seeing and sign-ing the targets.
- In the form of generic advice, identify three of the most common errors/weaknesses from any written assessed work set and feed these didactically back to the class.

Idea 9.11

Devise a self-assessment checklist for essays

This activity gets students to self-evaluate any essay they submit before you mark it, providing you with an invaluable opportunity to assess their ability to review and evaluate their own work. Devise a pro forma checklist that includes the fol-lowing questions: does the introduction address the question set? Does the introduction use key concepts? Does the main body start in a logical place? Does the main body answer the question? Does the writing flow logically? Are all key concepts used correctly and defined? Is there enough evidence of evaluation? Does each point made have an example to back it up? Is there adequate depth? Is it up to date? Is SPAG (spelling and grammar) of a sufficient standard? Get learners to run through any piece of writing they have done for you and tick which of the above criteria they have included.

Idea 9.12

Peer reviewing essays

Using the checklist devised in Idea 9.11, ask learners to swap essays and use those questions to assess each other's work. Based on what is and is not ticked, students write down three targets for future work. They must then submit this pro forma attached to the work they have done. When marking their work you will focus on their pro forma rather than the work they have done for you, assessing to what extent they have been good at evaluating their own work.

Idea 9.13
Talk it through

Very often students write summaries/essays/reports without necessarily understanding what it is they have written. Put students in groups to read their work to each other, but instruct each member of the group to stop the reader at any point and explain the point they are making in their own words. This experience will sharpen the evaluation skills of both readers and listeners, and flag up the importance of comprehension when submitting written work. For EAL learners, reading work out to others can be an invaluable experience, particularly if they have to explain what they have written in their own words.

Idea 9.14
Create a model answer

This activity will work well if the work to be assessed can be 'modelled' by looking at an exemplar (for example, an extended essay/picture/report that can be cut up, laminated and put into envelopes to be given to paired students). Give students the envelope with the exemplar and ask them to re-order it so that it makes logical sense, getting them to identify five characteristics that define why this piece of work warrants being an exemplar (be prepared to have your own defining characteristics to hand). Then ask students to evaluate their own work using the characteristics that the class have come up with. They then must decide on five targets they must deploy when next completing a piece of work.

Idea 9.15
Signposting evaluation

Learners often find writing structured, logically coherent paragraphs one of the most difficult skills to master. Ask learners to highlight the first word/words in each paragraph of their answers (and, if you really want to ram home the point, ask them to identify a midpoint in each paragraph). Then ask them to choose one or more of the evaluation phrases from the list below to add/substitute with the words they have highlighted:

The relevance of this; this indicates; this is similar to/different from; thus; so; therefore; this means/does not mean; hence; a consequence of; the implication of;

the contrast between; put simply; illustrated by; support for this; as shown by; this can be seen in; for example; this can be applied to; this is associated with; this leads to; this touches on; according to: the same applies to; this is confirmed by; in defence of this; a strength of this is; the value of; a benefit of; the usefulness of; an argument for; an advantage of; the importance of; this contributes to; this provides a balance to; this is significant because; this takes account of; however; alternatively; a criticism; another view; I disagree because; a different interpretation; on the other hand; the problem with this is; it is debatable; this is questioned; an argument against; a disadvantage of; although; this assumes; whereas; this cannot be explained by; this does not stand up because; this lacks support because; on the contrary; it makes little sense because; it is not true/valid because; to sum up; having weighed up; the balance of the argument suggests; the weight of evidence suggests; the conclusion is; I agree because; returning to the question.

Best practice – minimize the amount of work to be marked

While learners will require written feedback from you it is not necessary to do this all of the time. The following assessment activities require little or no marking but can, nevertheless, provide invaluable information about your learners:

Bringing in newspaper articles; choreographing a dance relating to a key issue; designing a leaflet/banner/poster; producing a photomontage; attaching summaries to highlighted texts; taking photographs with mobile telephones; producing tests/puzzles/quizzes for other class members to do; writing cartoon images for a theme; designing spider diagrams; bringing in artefacts/objects; designing a coat of arms; writing a short scene/sketch; bringing in 'examination' ready folders; assembling all homework for the year in chronological/thematic order; designing essay plans that can then be peer marked; creating revision posters/mindmaps to be displayed on walls of classroom; providing and distributing a list of 'top 10' websites to other learners explaining and reviewing their effectiveness.

Questions for professional development

1. What is your philosophy of assessment? The types of categories that you include in your mark book/records of assessment speak volumes about the sort of teacher you are, what you consider important and why. Develop your own thoughts about what is and what is not important when assessing the needs of your own learners and recognize that there is more to assessment than just measuring the academic output of learners.

2. Frequent examinations and tests with 'high stakes' often lead to demotivated learners and can stop the very learning that it is supposed to be assessing. It is worth noting that England possesses, internationally, one of the highest drop-out rates of post-16 learners and that this is associated with the huge assessment burden that learners and teachers experience. How might we as teachers avoid the burden of assessment while at the same time being rigorous in our support of learners?

3. Many teachers are adopting a 'traffic light' approach to learner self-assessment and feedback, for example, with learners grading work or lessons according to red for difficult, amber for moderately OK and green for easy. To what extent do you believe this is appropriate? What do you and your colleagues feel about introducing this aspect of 'learner voice' into assessment of learning?

4. Predicted grades (what a teacher thinks a learner will get from a test/examination), aspirational grades (what a learner is working towards) and minimum target grades (norm referenced against the rest of the national cohort) are commonly used in schools and some colleges. What criticisms can you identify in their usage? How can you adapt your practice to ensure that such criticism is not warranted?

Checklist: building your toolbox

- Teacher workload can prohibit quality feedback in many cases, so it is important to find strategies to cope with the mark load while giving sufficient feedforward to your learners. Using your mark book, target four or five students to whom you will give slightly more detailed comments every time you mark homework, and alternate this on a regular basis so that all learners get quality feedback from you regularly.

- Develop a range of peer-assessment strategies and introduce this very early on in your teaching so that learners get used to the benefits of this form of ipsative and formative assessment.

- Buy an old-fashioned mark book and/or develop an electronic equivalent on your own laptop. Ensure that this version contains within it all the categories that you deem to be essential above and beyond those associated with your institution. Tick off those that you use and work new categories into your practice on a regular basis.

- Try to ensure that a variety of your homework strategies are those that can be used as 'starter' activities and immediately peer assessed. The immediacy and relevance of this sort of activity will raise its profile in the minds of your learners and ease your assessment workload.

- Develop your own pro forma assessment sheets that incorporate the traffic light scheme (see Chapter 3) and are fit for purpose, with a variety of your own assessment strategies you use on a more regular basis (for example, presentations, essays, summaries).
- Providing you first seek permission from personal tutors, ring parents/ guardians the first time homework is not completed. This can be a gentle call to check that all is in place and that the student has not experienced difficulties: however, the call will quickly establish your reputation as a caring, meticulous and thorough practitioner who expects all work set to be done by deadline.

Chapter links

The ideas in this chapter relate closely with those also explored in Chapters 3, 4, 5 and 10.

Further reading

Assessment Reform Group (1999) *Assessment for Learning: Beyond the Black Box.* Cambridge: University of Cambridge School of Education.
Do not underestimate the impact of this tiny text. It is part of a body of work that has changed the educational landscape.

CHAPTER 10

HOMEWORK? STRATEGIES FOR LEARNING OUTSIDE OF THE CLASSROOM

Chapter overview

The aims of the chapter are to:

1. Incorporate the use of e-learning in homework strategies.
2. Provide a range of differentiated homework ideas.
3. Provide advice and guidance on what to do when learners do not complete homework tasks.
4. Suggest homework strategies that reduce the burden of marking.

Problem-solving

The title of this chapter reflects our passion for 'homework' as a learning strategy while accepting that for many learners, conditions at home are such that this strategy is unrealistic and impossible to achieve. 'Homework' is therefore not something that we necessarily advocate being done at home. When creatively and considerately deployed, homework can be carried out anywhere, can promote independent learning, assist in the development of generic skills and can free up time for further work on any curriculum (Hallam, 2000). But homework is not just a strategy for raising achievement. When skilfully deployed, it can instil passion, motivation and enthusiasm for the subject in the hearts and minds of your learners. However, as experienced teachers ourselves, we also recognize how homework can often be a site of anxiety between parents, schools/colleges and many teenagers.

Context

The case for the use of homework as a strategy to enhance learning is contentious. Many researchers (for example, Soloman et al., 2002; Walker et al., 2004) argue that homework can have a negative impact on family life by adding to the tensions that already exist between parents and teenagers. These tensions can be exacerbated when some parents view homework as an opportunity for their children to make up for failures they themselves experienced when they were pupils. Others feel that they lack sufficient knowledge, skills and time to be able to support their children and feel alienated from their pupils and the teachers that teach them. Nevertheless, we know that homework can boost achievement providing it stimulates and challenges, it is done in moderate amounts, learners understand its nature and purpose, it is doable, and is marked and returned to learners quickly. Epstein (1988) has outlined seven purposes that homework fulfils: the practising of skills; increasing learning-task involvement; fostering the personal development of the learner (for example, motivation; self-confidence); establishing and strengthening communication between parents and students; satisfying government and school policy expectations/requirements; and in some cases the punishment of pupils. Needless to say, we wholeheartedly reject this last purpose. The Children's Act states that homework should always be 'meaningful' and never set as punishment. Properly structured and facilitated homework can add one year to a student's full-time education (Stern, 2009). It can promote individual pride and success in learners and can often generate the most creative and memorable work a student ever does (for example, that project; that podcast; that painting; that prize-winning essay). Finally, homework provides you, the teacher, with invaluable evidence of learner engagement with your subject and your teaching strategies. As such, it is an invaluable source of summative, formative and ipsative assessment of your teaching.

Creativity, energy and openness are the hallmarks of a great teacher. The following suggestions for homework strategies are underpinned by a range of educational theories on learning as well as expert practice that we have witnessed in many of the schools and colleges we regularly visit. We have tried to include suggestions that offer a variety of assessment opportunities but, above all, we have tried to ensure that these ideas motivate and energize your learners. Experiment with them and adapt them to your own practice.

Toolbox

Homework for 'digital natives'

The following ideas incorporate a variety of e-learning technologies, most of which should be available and accessible to learners within all schools and colleges (see Chapter 7 for further discussion of these ideas). As with all learning activities, these need to be carefully scaffolded by teachers but remember that most teenagers have grown up in an environment where they quickly adapt to, and master, new technologies. Harnessing this enthusiasm and applying it to any homework strategy will transform the learning experience in and outside the classroom.

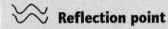 **Reflection point**

The emergence of new technology related to e-learning has led, some claim, to so called 'digital natives', that is, someone who is completely comfortable with using this technology. That said, it is extremely important that you diagnose, differentiate and support learners with their e-literacy. In Chapter 7 we deal more fully with this topic. While we strongly advocate the use of e-learning strategies when teaching, we would also ask you to reflect on how the addition of an e-learning strategy enhances the learning experience of your students.

Best practice – digital safety

The Byron Review (DCSF, 2008) identifies codes of safe practice for parents and educators supporting children learning with digital and virtual worlds. This report was written in the light of understandable anxiety concerning high-volume Internet, social networking and SMS (text messaging) usage among the young. The report concludes that digital and virtual worlds offer enriching learning experiences but only if managed correctly. The report notes that while children and young people have a huge capacity for quickly developing confidence with emerging technologies, their critical skills need further support to help them make appropriate decisions regarding their e-safety. The full review can be downloaded from www.dcsf.gov.uk/byronreview.

Idea 10.1

Making posters with Glogster.com

Glogster.com allows you to mix graphics, photographs, music, videos and text into a variety of formats which can then be posted up for others to see as an interactive poster. Items can be highlighted and tagged with direct links to any image, sound or text. Get learners to create posters that draw together the speeches, moving images, newspaper reports and reportage on any theme related to your subject. This can be done at the beginning of a unit as a way of drawing learners into the subject, or at the end as a summary and revision source for public examinations.

Idea 10.2

Diigo chain

Diigo stands for Digest of Internet Information, Groups and Other Stuff and is one of the most recent social book-marking spaces. When you highlight a word on any page on the Internet a dropdown menu appears that allows you to search for highlighted words on the Web, bookmarking systems, blogs, and so on. Visually it offers a stunning way for students to follow research trajectories. Set up a group for your class, asking them to research a particular topic. Each learner must put three relevant links up on Diigo. This homework allows you to see instantly how students are engaging with their subject and it provides a fabulous resource for all learners in that group.

Idea 10.3

Moviemaker trailer

Moviemaker allows you to create stunning short films based on any moving images you have recorded or downloaded. You can incorporate text, subtitles, credits, and so on in professional formats, and it is straightforward to use. Get students in pairs to produce a short film/documentary (maximum of 5 minutes' duration) that introduces your subject or a topic you choose for new learners. They can be as imaginative as they like but they must incorporate key concepts, names and so on as well as common forms of assessment. Offer a prize for the best film and tell them that their film will be used in school/college open evenings for prospective students.

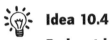 **Idea 10.4**

Podcast journalism

In Chapter 7 we explain how to make podcasts. Pair learners up, making sure they have access to a flipcam or any equivalent filming device. Learners must take it in turns to film each other reporting on a major event. This must be in the formal style of a foreign correspondent reporting on a major issue. This could be a historical/current event and can be linked to any character/event that is relevant to your topic area. Podcasts can then be uploaded and made available to all learners. A prize can be awarded to the 'Best Reporter' on the basis of votes from all those participating.

 Idea 10.5

Google Earthopologist

This activity will foster curiosity and a sense of adventure. Give students a destination and ask them to explore this with Google Earth. Get them to take screen shots of any location relevant (for example, they could explore the slums in Jakarta or Rio de Janeiro from the point of view of an anthropologist/ foreign correspondent). They must make diary entries on what they see and 'experience' and then report these back to the class as they display their screen shots.

 Idea 10.6

Debating with Yammer

This micro-blogging tool allows you to post short comments/updates (like Twitter) but in a safer environment in that all users have to share the school or institution email address. Set up two teams in your class and get them to debate on line, with each class member posting a comment based on a contentious issue. Ensure that each comment must alternate between Team A and Team B. Once all postings are in set an essay to all learners based on the comments that have been made.

Idea 10.7

Teaching your grandmother

Learners will require mobile phones or any visual recording equipment for this activity. Ask students to go home and teach their parents/guardians/grandparents a key concept/theme that has been taught in class the same day. The learner must be filmed by a member of their family giving the explanation and this film brought in to the next lesson. The teacher can pick at random films to be seen/shown. Alternatively the activity can be backed up with a signature from the guardian/parent to show that this activity has taken place.

Best practice – speaking to parents

If at all possible, talk to parents and try to find out whether or not pupils have the right sort of working conditions they require to carry out homework at home. Offer alternatives (for example, homework clubs; library space; early arrival and use of classroom space) if such conditions are not available at home. Find out what the school homework policy is and talk this through with parents. If necessary devise a 'homework guidance sheet' to include the following: student responsibility re homework (for example, deadlines; presentation); what is expected from parents/guardians regarding homework (checking that the work is done; signing of homework diaries; the role of parental praise); how the nature of homework will change as learners progress through school/college; the ideal working environment (for example, computer; ventilation; heating; book shelves; lack of distraction); advice/guidance on time management.

Best practice – a warning about e-learning

Adopting e-learning approaches comes with a pedagogic 'health warning'. In this age of rapidly expanding and changing web tools, platforms and services, there are no guarantees that the tools of today will not be defunct by tomorrow. Therefore, be very careful when investing time in preparing niche and bespoke e-learning objects to ensure they are as future–proof and scaleable as possible. When planning lessons and learning outcomes based on these tools, ensure that all learners have appropriate access (especially important if used as homework/outside of the classroom learning). If used in the classroom ensure you have non-technological back-ups.

Multiple intelligence and homework

Ongoing research on multiple intelligences contests the idea that intelligence is determined by somebody's 'IQ'. Instead, 'intelligences' take many forms that can include: linguistic, logical mathematical, musical, spatial, bodily kinaesthetic, naturalist, interpersonal, intrapersonal and existential. As a strategy for differentiation, the following homework ideas embrace a range of these intelligences and will appeal to those who find traditional forms of homework uninspiring.

 Idea 10.8

A day in the life

The use of empathy can be a powerful tool in getting students to appreciate the different historical and geographical contexts related to their subject area. Ask learners to write a diary entry related to a key person in your subject domain. Get them to empathize as much as possible with the person, their locality and the historical context in which the entry is being written.

 Idea 10.9

Newspaper editor

Introduce learners to one of the many publishing packages available on their computers. Get them to design the front cover of their favourite newspaper – ideally this works best with one of the broadsheets. They must pick all the stories and pictures from other sources but must write the lead article (maximum 200 words). This can be done in pairs but works best if given as a solo activity.

 Idea 10.10

Street photography

Mobile phones are powerful teaching aids and often go underused as a teaching resource. Ask students to use their mobile phones as cameras on their way home. They must take five photographs of items that directly relate to your subject area and then must present these to the class, justifying why they have chosen to take these photographs.

Idea 10.11

Making a spectacle of yourself

This task works well if your subject consists of theories/approaches/different perspectives on how to analyse your topic areas. Get students to make a pair of glasses. These can be as ornate and as decorated as possible but must reflect a particular approach (for example, Marxist glasses might have words like 'class', 'power', 'inequality' and might be decorated with pictures of Engels, Lenin, and so on). Get students to make these at home and bring them in. Then watch the fun as they swap their glasses in class and have to argue their topic/subject through the 'lenses' of the particular perspective.

Idea 10.12

Modelling

This homework will spill over into classwork and will require you to have a range of model-making accessories (scissors, glue, Blu-Tack). Ask learners in pairs/threes to bring in any items from home (this works brilliantly with items of garbage, for example, crushed drink cans). Their job in your class will be to create a model of any concept related to your subject area (for example, a symbol, a building, a tool). Prizes can go to the best model and you should ensure that the models go on show within the school/college.

Reflection point

Education research on homework indicates that, in many institutions: high-ability students will be set larger amounts of homework; many students feel that teacher expectations are one of the most decisive factors in motivating learners to complete homework; learners need homework to be directly linked to the lesson; many teachers view homework as something that reinforces, reviews and practises the content/concepts/theories taught in their lessons; homework is often hurriedly set within the last 5 minutes of the lesson, and in many cases after the lesson has ended, with instructions rushed and unclear; a significant amount of homework carried out by students is left unmarked; there is a point at which more time spent on homework has a negative effect on learning; the longer it takes for homework to be marked and returned to students the less effective it is as a source of assessment.

(Continued)

(Continued)

In light of all of the above points, reflect on how you can enhance your homework strategies. Revisit your schemes of work and see how you can restructure them in ways that maximize the effectiveness of the homework you set.

 Idea 10.13

Snakes and ladders

Get students, in pairs, to design a snakes and ladders board game. The 'snakes' and the 'ladders' scenarios must be directly related to your subject area and must contain within them events, characters and key concepts that strictly apply to what they are studying. They must create snake-and-ladder scenarios that encapsulate dilemmas within their own subject domain. The advantage of this is that the games can then be used in the class as starter activities or as a light-hearted but poignant break from the lesson. This activity can be applied to a variety of well-known board games.

 Idea 10.14

Photomontage

While technology has come on in leaps and bounds in recent years, remember that students often enjoy being creative with 'real' artwork as opposed to 'virtual'. Give students a particular theme related to your subject area and then instruct them to create a photomontage using images from magazines, newspapers, the Internet, labels from grocery items. Students need to write a short description as to what and why the images represent the concept(s).

 Idea 10.15

Content analysis

Give students a range of newspapers that they have to buy/read over a period of time. Ensure that the theme is worthy of photojournalistic content. Get them to measure the space occupied in the paper for certain categories of photograph (for example, pictures of sports men and women; criminality). Get them to write up their findings discussing why they believe that less/more space is given to certain topics in the media.

Idea 10.16

Creative writing

Give students the opportunity to create fiction that is related to your own topic. Ask them to: write letters to politicians/agony aunts or anybody famous about a theme that worries them; write a diary entry of a day in the life of somebody famous; write a CV about themselves either 50 years in the past or 20 years in the future.

Idea 10.17

Let there be music

Music can be a powerful incentive for many teenagers when it comes to their own subject areas. Learners can be asked to create a 'top 20' list of song titles that relate to your topic area. Learners can be asked to take any piece of contemporary music that is likely to be popular with most of your learners. Ask them to rewrite two verses of the song to include key concepts from your subject area. Alternatively, get students to write a jingle using key concepts from your subject.

 Reflection point

Time management for teachers and students is an essential factor in the success of homework as a teaching and learning strategy. As you develop your homework strategies, consider and reflect on the following questions: should you set a certain amount of time to be spent on homework and accept that different students will produce different amounts? Alternatively, should you set a task knowing that it will take learners different amounts of time to complete it? In considering these questions what sorts of strategies do you have in place when students fail to hand work in on time? How and when should you collect homework in? Departmental homework policies and schemes of work will, to a certain extent, help you with these dilemmas but it is also important for you, as a professional, to develop your own emerging philosophy around these issues.

Homework that maximizes the impact of your marking time

While we fully understand the need for formative assessment and its relationship to specific targets set when marking homework, we also realize the immense workload that teachers face. Not all homework necessarily needs direct feedback from teachers. The trick is to make sure that homework is completed by all students, while ensuring that the homework is both meaningful and informs their future progress in the subject. The following ideas can be woven into your overall homework strategy. They cannot replace more traditional forms of homework (for example, essays, presentations, summaries and so on) but can enhance your repertoire while creating meaningful learning opportunities for your students.

 Idea 10.18

Multiple choice

Get students to create 20 questions with 20 separate sets of answers (four answers to each question, of which only one is correct). When students come into your next lesson, pair them up and get them to do each other's multiple choice tests. This activity can be varied to include homemade crosswords, true/false quizzes, anagrams, and so on.

 Idea 10.19

Mark it up and summarize

Give students a set reading/article/chapter and get them to highlight key words in the text. They must bring this into class and have attached to it a 200-word summary. Students must then verbally summarize to the class the content of the article. This works best when different articles have been assigned to different groups within your class.

 Idea 10.20

Flash cards

If your subject is one in which a public examination is part of the course, get students very early on in the course to start creating their own revision/flash cards. These can be done periodically, reflecting various stages of the course. It is important that they look aesthetically pleasing (special prizes can be given for the best-looking cards). The cards can then be brought in and used in a variety of ways (for example, students test each other; they can be placed on a pro forma you have created with specific categories).

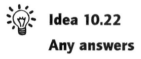

Idea 10.21
Revision

You will need model answers for this particular revision task. Set four essay titles for homework (ensuring that you have model answers for each). Each learner must produce a plan for each essay. Students then come into your class knowing that they will write, under timed conditions, one of the essays but they will not know which one until you set it. Give students 10 minutes in groups of four to discuss each of their plans and then choose one essay title for them to write up under timed conditions. After they have completed this, 'reward them' with the four model answers and give them the opportunity (with an examiner's mark scheme) to peer mark their work.

Idea 10.22

Any answers

Get students to write down five questions based on any area of the curriculum that you have just taught. This can be based on readings/research/activities but your learners must also write down the correct answers to their own questions and must learn these answers off by heart. When students come in to your next lesson simply stand back and ask the first student to fire their own questions at other class members who have to respond. The first student to correctly answer a question must then ask their questions to the class, and so on.

Best practice – tackling non-completion of homework

Sometimes it is not possible, despite all our best intentions, for some learners to carry out homework tasks. There are a variety of reasons for this that include lack of space and privacy at home; family pressures; lack of understanding of the tasks set; an inability to take down the correct instructions; not having the correct resources; alienation and disengagement from school processes; and a lack of time due to other hobbies/interests/priorities. Consider the following strategies for dealing with non-completion of homework: using the library as a place for homework; do homework at a friend's house; recommend a lock for the bedroom

(Continued)

(Continued)

door; getting up early in the morning when it's quiet; borrowing extra resources from school; asking teachers to write down/email instructions; check eyesight; refer them to outside interested bodies regarding specific deadline dates (for example, parents' evenings; reports; examination boards); ensure homework instructions are not set in the final few minutes of the lesson; be consistent with punitive action (for example, if you say you will give a detention then follow this through); offer prizes for best homework; monitor homework diaries; mark homework regularly and return it quickly; involve learning assistants in the setting of homework and build them into your schemes of work.

Questions for professional development

1. How often do you update your own knowledge about new sites/resources related to your own subject? When was the last time you logged into your own subject association's website? You will be amazed at how many resources are available from most subject associations which are free and easy to access from home/school/college.
2. How regularly do you ask students to give you feedback on your teaching strategies, including the types of homework you set? Their views can be really useful in informing your future schemes of work. Find out from them the types of homework activities they really enjoy from other teachers and see if you can build some of their strategies into your own teaching.
3. Do you record when you set homework and the date that you give it back? Aim to give back homework as quickly as possible to students. You will find that the quicker you return work the greater the participation of all your students in the tasks you set them.
4. Are you aware of when in the lesson you set work? Make a mental note from now on as to when you set homework tasks and ensure that you aim to set homework very early in the lesson. By doing this you will scaffold the lesson and students will focus more on your content, on the assumption that this will feed into their homework tasks.

Checklist: building your toolbox

While there is much that you can do to raise expectations and the importance of homework in the eyes of your learners we also accept that the most successful institutions are these where there is considerable inter-departmental coordination and discussion about the purpose, timing, level of difficulty, availability of resources and range of activities associated with homework. In addition to the ideas in this chapter we recommend the following:

- Create a homework league table and offer a prize at the end of each half-term for the top three students.
- Coordinate homework with other teachers/departments (refer to your schemes of work (SOWs)).
- Be meticulous in recording what homework was set and when in your mark book/assessment records.
- Photocopy the occasional page of homework to send home to parents.
- Make sure that all homework activities are seen by learners as relevant; useful and doable.
- Do not be afraid to ring parents about homework. Many parents value the opportunity to speak with teachers about this and you will quickly get a reputation with students as a result.
- Monitor homework diaries and make sure you are in regular contact with tutors/year heads/faculty managers, keeping them informed.

Chapter links

The ideas in this chapter relate closely with those also explored in Chapters 4, 5, 7 and 9.

Further reading

Hallam, S. (2000) *Homework: The Evidence*. London: Institute of Education.
In Sue Hallam's book we are alerted to the benefits of homework while being warned of the potential pitfalls.

CHAPTER **11**

CHALLENGING LEARNERS OF ALL ABILITIES

Chapter overview

The aims of the chapter are to:

1. Illustrate what differentiation and personalization are and why they are important for motivation.
2. Provide examples of differentiation strategies that can be deployed to support divergent learners.
3. Illustrate ideas for stretching and challenging learners.
4. Demonstrate the relationships between classroom climate, differentiation and motivation.

Problem-solving

When we talk about 'differentiation' we refer to the ways in which teachers plan and teach to cater for individual needs. The idea is that we treat learners individually as a means to target support to increase their learning and potential to learn. The notion of 'personalization' is how the idea of differentiation appears in the government discourse in the teacher standards for secondary sector teachers.

Irrespective of the language and discourse adopted – the notion that teachers need to cater for learners' needs and all learners need to be stretched and challenged is essential for motivating and engagement.

When UK teachers, managers and policy-makers have talked about 'stretch' and 'challenge' there is sometimes (and this has been perhaps more true in the past) the assumption that we are talking about stretching and challenging the more able of our learners (the 'gifted and talented'). While this is clearly very important (and often missing from individual teachers' lesson planning), we must stretch and challenge *all* our learners – to support them in the 'distance travelled' through individual lessons and through longer-term learning journeys. We need to challenge learners and help support them to achieve the challenges we place before them. Activities which are too easy are as demotivating as work which is too hard. This means that planning for 'personalization' or 'differentiation' is essential – and we need to undertake this planning based upon astute and well-evidenced assessments of prior learning. We need to encourage learners to take risks but help them to achieve. Risk-taking which leads to learners failing is sometimes highly demotivating. Equally, as we ask our learners to experiment and take risks, teachers need to take risks and experiment too. The Office for Standards in Education (Ofsted) note that one of the characteristics of an 'outstanding' teacher is the ability to take risks in the classroom and to plan and perform lessons which stretch all learners. This challenge also needs to inform learners' own assessments of their abilities and progress – what we call 'assessment for learning' (see Chapters 3 and 9) and their meta-cognition (see Chapter 12). Such challenging learning – if done supportively and successfully – can have a huge impact upon the classroom climate (see Chapter 5). Equally, differentiation and personalization themselves can have a massive impact on how teachers plan, how learners self-assess, how learners work cooperatively with others and how the climate of social relations in the classroom feels.

Context

In their research paper *Testing, Motivation and Learning* the Assessment Reform Group (2002) highlights the interrelationships between motivation, effort and self-esteem. In their 'motivation for learning' approach (linked to the wider 'assessment for learning' approach outlined in Chapters 3 and 9) it is believed that self-esteem affects how one sees one's ability to be able to learn. This is called 'self-efficacy' – how 'capable' learners feel in achieving and succeeding at their learning. Self-efficacy in turn affects effort – how much one is prepared to try something and continue to try before giving up. The implications of all this are that we need to support learners to feel they can try and take risks, but we must be conscious of how important success is. Learner failure could lead to a lack of effort, which itself might then affect the likelihood of success. 'Low achievers' need a high level of input and support from both home and school/college to escape from this cycle. This report also notes that the degree to which learners can take control of their own learning (and make their own choices about their learning) has a positive effect on learning outcomes – and can really extend learning for learners of all abilities.

Toolbox

You can differentiate by . . .

All of the above context has tremendous implications for differentiation and personalization and the role they play in the classroom. In this section, we provide a series of practical ideas for you to try, which enable differentiation to take place. It is essential that this is built into lesson planning and preparation processes. Each of these strategies is a different way to differentiate and would help support a diverse range of learners, irrespective of their abilities. Many are based upon the assumption that you 'know your learners' and can clearly identify their needs – usually based upon continued and ongoing assessments of prior learning.

Best practice – differentiation by using 'Bloom's taxonomy'

Writing in the mid to late 1950s cognitive psychologist Bloom (1956a) developed a theory of learning and thinking which saw learning as operating across three 'domains' – the cognitive (thinking), the psycho-motor (physical 'doing') and the affective (relationships and emoting) domains. Within each of these three types or 'domains' of learning there exists a 'hierarchy' – a series of levels which develop up from 'surface' to 'deep' learning. In the cognitive domain we have:

- knowledge;
- comprehension;
- application;
- analysis;
- synthesis;
- evaluation.

Anderson and Krathwohl (2001) have taken the notion of a hierarchy or taxonomy of 'thinking skills', extending Bloom, and instead offer:

- remembering;
- understanding;
- applying;
- analysing;
- evaluating;
- creating.

All of these models are excellent sources for differentiation – they provide ways for teachers and learners to identify skills, 'locate' their learning on a hierarchy of levels and have a means by which they can think about what skills they have, and what they need to work on next. Consider Ideas 11.1 to 11.4 for some examples of this.

Idea 11.1

. . . using Bloom 1

Try opening lessons using Bloom's cognitive domain as a means to scaffold questions to the group. As you move through Bloom's hierarchy the questions get harder as they move from surface to deeper learning. You could ask different 'levels' of questions to different learners or see how far individuals can get through the whole scaffold.

Idea 11.2

. . . using Bloom 2

Introduce learners to the terminology of Bloom's cognitive domain and get them to understand what the levels mean and how these map against their own skills and abilities. Get them to audit their own skills using written work as a means for them to 'evidence' what skills they are demonstrating and where. They could use different coloured pens and highlighters to mark where the different skills are in their work as a means to self-assess.

Idea 11.3

. . . using Bloom 3

Try a Bloom's 'circuit training' classroom set-up (see also Idea 4.4). Provide a number of different tables as 'islands' with different tasks on. Identify with a place name (maybe laminated so you can reuse them) the Bloom's skill of the table. Some will be 'knowledge', some 'synthesis', and so on. Allow learners to choose (and support them in doing so) which tables and combinations of island activities they complete based upon their own assessment of their skills and needs.

Reflection point

The language of Bloom's cognitive domain is certainly familiar to most teachers – it is the language of most key stage attainment targets, examination board grading schemes and marking. This language has permeated the UK education system and is often the means by which we assess learners' progress and the outcomes of their work. Think about how often you see these terms on schemes of work and mark schemes. What does this mean for marking, assessment and for categorizing learners' needs? How might you draw upon this language in making assessments of learners' skills and work, and how might you make these transparent to learners?

Idea 11.4

. . . using Bloom 4

Prepare your lesson so that you have six separate activities – one each for each level of Bloom's cognitive domain – knowledge, comprehension, application, analysis, synthesis, evaluation (maybe 12 very small activities if you wish to do two per the levels of Bloom). Arrange the classroom so that each task is lined up in order along a wall. Learners (in pairs or groups) start working at the lowest level and see how far they can progress through the tasks; you check at each stage before allowing them to continue on to the next one.

Best practice – specialist support that is 'good for all'

According to the General Teaching Council's (GTC's) 2008 research report 'Research for teachers: strategies for supporting dyslexic learners' it was suggested that up to 1 in 20 learners are likely to have dyslexia. What is perhaps really interesting about these claims is the 'specialist advice' provided to support such learners – as summarized below:

1. Get learners to see connections between things.
2. Help learners to remember learning as a journey with a pattern so the connections between bits of knowledge are clear.
3. Patterns are more important that mere sequences.
4. See the larger patterns – think holistically.
5. Apply learning to practical experience so the point of the learning is made clear (GTC, 2008: 2).

Although this specialist support is hugely important to get right, nonetheless, this is a clear example of where all learners might benefit from the differentiation strategies applied to targeted dyslexic learners. The list above is essentially about providing structure to enable learning to take place effectively.

 Idea 11.5

. . . materials

Learners study different materials with roughly the same content and they do the same tasks (using the different materials they have). The materials might vary in terms of language, presentation, size of text, colour of background, but the actual content is the same, it is the accessibility of the materials and its presentation of information that varies.

 Idea 11.6

. . . content

Learners study different materials with different content. The issue or work in question could be more detailed and less detailed depending upon the learner. It could have harder questions (see Bloom's taxonomy above) or easier questions. It could even have more work to do for some, and less for others. What the learners get is based upon assessments of their prior learning and skills either undertaken by the teacher or by the learner themselves.

Idea 11.7

. . . extension

When doing lessons structured by a series of group-work activities ensure you always have an extension activity for those groups who finish early. This extension could be presented to them as a 'secret extra task'. Ensure that the task itself is meaningful, stretches the more able, but at the same time is not essential for all (otherwise everyone should be doing it anyway).

Best practice – a summary of differentiation strategies

1. You can ask different learners different questions or ask the same questions in different ways.
2. You can give different amounts of time to complete the same tasks depending upon need.
3. You can set up peer groups differently according to either mixing abilities or matching needs of learners.
4. You can vary the length of time you support different learners for.
5. You can vary the nature of the support you offer learners.
6. Different learners could choose what tasks they do (with your guidance and support).
7. Different learners could choose how they present or undertake a task.
8. You could even choose to let learners make choices or to set them for them.

 Reflection point

We started this chapter by saying that learners need to be encouraged to take risks and to experiment – and that teachers need to as well. Why not use differentiation as the basis for reflective work with colleagues? You could plan with others to try out a series of different differentiation strategies and then track and measure their impact and effectiveness. Try to also include learners' voices in the measurement of this impact. This could be a very useful and interesting 'action research' strategy that would merit being shared across your institution.

What might the barriers to differentiation be for your practice? Differentiation is not easy; it involves very careful manipulation of a number of elements in your planning and preparation. It is also not easy as there are sometimes some barriers to achieving successful differentiation, such as:

- size of class;
- frequency of contact with the group;
- lack of materials for extension and support;
- lack of specialist staff to support and guide.

How might these barriers affect you? How might you overcome them?

 Idea 11.8

. . . role

When organizing groups and group membership, give different learners different roles – scribe, chair, feedback, and so on. You can rotate the roles lesson by lesson and also try to give learners different roles to extend and develop their skill-set over time.

 Idea 11.9

. . . support 1

You can differentiate and stretch learners by the amount of support you give them – either in groups or as individuals. Some learners will need more support than others; some will need to be encouraged to be more 'independent' as a means to stretch them.

 Idea 11.10

. . . support 2

You can differentiate by the type of support you give, not just the amount (see Idea 11.9 above). Some learners might need to be coaxed into 'getting the right answer' whereas others might need to be challenged and extended with higher-level questioning. Some might need to be given clues, others to be left to be more independent (although you need to explain to them why you might not be answering their questions).

Idea 11.11

. . . support 3

You can differentiate the type of support materials you allow individuals and groups to use to aid them with the completion of a task. Some might be allowed dictionaries, others an Internet enabled PC, some textbooks or class notes, and so on.

 Idea 11.12

. . . time

Do not be afraid of giving learners different amounts of time to complete either the same or different activities. Establish the sort of climate whereby you can say to groups 'I want you to finish this in 10 minutes'. And others 'I want you to finish this in 20 . . .'. It might feel like you are 'spinning plates' with different things going on at the same time, but it can really help you to target the needs of the learners if you do this.

 Idea 11.13

. . . free choice

Asking learners to make choices over the work they do and the activities they engage in is very empowering. It increases their 'locus of control'. You can also ask learners to choose how long they might take over a task or even how they might present a finished outcome. This is an excellent opportunity to talk to learners, discuss their skills and encourage them to explore control over their own learning.

 Idea 11.14

. . . negotiation

As opposed to giving a 'free choice' (see Idea 11.13 above), you could negotiate: 'You can choose what you do next as long as you do task one first' or 'Tell me which three tasks you would like to do today, but explain why you have made the choice you have'. As with Idea 11.13, these examples allow learners to develop their 'locus of control' over their own learning and also are a means to 'personalize' learning and learning outcomes.

Idea 11.15

. . . grouping

A classic way to differentiate is by planning very specifically the group membership for learners. You could mix abilities together or you could organize learners of similar abilities together or even keep with 'friendship groups'. Which of these options you choose might depend upon which other types of differentiation you adopt from the ideas above.

Taking learners to the 'next step'

As well as supporting learners and their needs, we need to then extend them beyond the place where they currently are in their learning. This is why 'challenging' learners is so vital – and why issues of differentiation, support and challenge go hand in hand.

 Idea 11.16

Using the 'six thinking hats'.

This idea uses some 'thinking tools' discussed in more depth in Chapter 12 where we explore Edward de Bono's idea of 'six thinking hats' more fully. Ask learners to contribute in group work tasks according to one of the six thinking hats devised by de Bono (see page 155). Try and stretch learners to adopt ways and strategies of thinking that they would not normally adopt.

 Idea 11.17

Lateral thinking

Following on from the ideas presented in Idea 11.16, it is important to encourage learners to develop 'alternatives' in their thinking. This is, in part, what it means to think 'laterally' – to try to develop different ways to see and approach the same issue or problem. Always stretch learners by asking them to think of 'other ways it could be . . .'. This could be a great starter to energize the group and stimulate them – a great way therefore to develop pace in the lesson from the very start. For example, show your group a newspaper article or a news clip of a

(Continued)

(Continued)

historic event and ask them to think how else it might have turned out; show them the outcome of a science experiment and ask them how things might be different if the experiment had not worked.

 Idea 11.18

Cognitive challenge

This idea is one of the suggestions made to start lessons in a 'thinking classroom' (see Chapter 12). Try to challenge learners by either presenting them with the opposite view to the one they hold, or by asking them to argue/think from the opposite view of the one they hold. Give them a 'cognitive shake-up' right at the start and capture their interest in the lesson.

 Idea 11.19

Socratic questioning

Try to stretch learners by adopting a 'Socratic questioning' approach. Do not ask open questions or closed questions (which limit response) but instead try and draw out higher-order thinking from learners as your interaction and questioning develops. Ask them questions such as:

- 'Why?'
- 'What do you mean by that?'
- 'Can you tell me more about that?'
- 'Why do you think that?'

 Reflection point

Think about how many of the above differentiation, challenging and personalization strategies you actually use in the classroom. How many do you do, and how many do you formally plan for and articulate on lesson planning documents? Think about the whole differentiation repertoire you have and add these strategies to your 'toolbox'.

Questions for professional development

1. What differentiation strategies do you currently use? How many are formally planned for and how many are just a part of your classroom teaching craft? Try and have a reflective and conscious command over all you do, and plan and target it appropriately for the personalization of the learners' needs.
2. How can you develop the challenge in your class, but support learners at the same time? How can you encourage them to take risks and stretch themselves?
3. How can you support your learners' 'locus of control'?
4. Which differentiation strategies would be most appropriate for your higher ability learners, and which for your less able? How do you move the latter forwards in their learning?

Checklist: building your toolbox

- Develop Socratic and Bloom-based questioning techniques to stretch learners.
- Plan for learners doing different things in different amounts of time.
- Build a variety of differentiation and personalization strategies into each lesson to ensure the lesson has pace and variety (this keeps learners engaged and on task, and also caters for their needs, which in turn is motivating).
- Develop Bloom's notion of deeper learning at the top of the cognitive domain as a means to extend and challenge learners at the higher end of the ability spectrum.
- Encourage learners to self-assess and to make choices and decisions about their learning.

Chapter links

The ideas in this chapter relate closely with those also explored in Chapters 3, 6 and 12.

Further reading

Muijs, D. and Reynolds, D. (2010) *Effective Teaching: Evidence and Practice*, 3rd edn. London: Sage.
Contains a really useful section on teaching and supporting 'gifted' learners.

CHAPTER 12

SUPPORTING LEARNERS IN LEARNING HOW TO LEARN

Chapter overview

The aims of the chapter are to:

1. Introduce the importance of meta-cognition for developing learners' learning and thinking skills.
2. Provide strategies for supporting learners' thinking skills both inside and outside the classroom.
3. Demonstrate approaches in developing learners' criticality.
4. Illustrate the role collaborative learning plays in developing learners' learning.

Problem-solving

We hear a great deal from the media about the 'dumbing-down' of examination requirements and the ease of assessment. These moral panics are usually timed to arrive during the summer when examination boards, schools and colleges release examination results from public examinations and assessments. One of the key aspects of this 'dumbing-down' argument is the suggested lack or decline of 'evaluation' skills. Whether one believes the view that 'exams are easier' and 'learners exercise their criticality' less, or not, it is the case that attention given to a wide range of thinking skills can really help support and develop learners' learning. In turn, 'thinking' itself (and getting 'better' at it) can be highly motivating if learners can see the progress they are making and understand for themselves the processes they are adopting. In this chapter we offer strategies for developing what various writers and practitioners have referred to as a 'thinking classroom' (McGuiness, 1999).

Context

What is 'thinking' and what is a 'thinking classroom'? At first glance, this seems obvious, does it not? All classrooms are thinking classrooms since learning takes place in them and thinking is needed for learning. However, by referring to the techniques and ideas in this chapter as producing a 'thinking classroom' we are saying that, as teachers, we perhaps need to plan and prepare for thinking more than we might currently do. Equally, we are saying that by concentrating on techniques for developing thinking, we can perhaps take something essential (which we might take for granted) and really give it the focus it deserves – exponentially developing learners' learning in the process.

Definitions of what exactly is thinking are contested – the concept is not as clear as we might think in our common-sense understandings. Having said this, much of the literature (see McGregor, 2007) points to the fact that thinking is 'cognitive' (to do with the mind) and that it is a process. The literature also shows that we can develop and improve thinking by practising it. Thinking is natural and occurs all the time, in all aspects of our daily lives, but this does not mean it is easy to do well. Having said this, the research and literature on thinking skills and strategies suggests that the more we practise thinking, and develop strategies for clear and effective thinking, then the greater the rewards we will receive from this ability. This means thinking is somehow both a skill and an ability all at the same time: we are able, biologically, to 'think' (we have an innate ability), and yet if we practise it, we get better at it (skill). Thinking about our own thinking – what we call meta-cognition – is perhaps the greatest skill and strategy of all, as it allows us to understand how we approach problems and solutions.

Edward De Bono says, 'The main difficulty of thinking is confusion. We try to do too much at once. Emotions, information, logic, hope and creativity all crowd in on us. It is like juggling with too many balls' (De Bono, 1985: xi). In terms of motivation, turning your lessons into 'thinking classrooms' enables learners to see the progress they are making with their thinking – allowing them to make even more progress and to see their own learning taking off. This is highly motivating.

Toolbox

Meta-cognition – towards a thinking classroom

When we talk of 'meta-cognition' we mean 'thinking about thinking', 'meta' referring to something above and beyond, looking down onto something else. Another way to explain the usefulness of this to both learning and the motivation to learn is to slightly change the definition to 'learning about learning'. In other words, if we can get learners to understand why and how they think and learn as they do, we can support them with longer-term strategies to develop this further.

Reflection point

There is a great deal of research that illustrates the links between motivation and meta-cognition. For example, the Assessment Reform Group's (2002) *Testing, Motivating and Learning* review demonstrates that meta-cognition is important for learners to gain a sense of their own self as a learner – a key ingredient for developing the 'motivation to learn'. How do you develop this in your own classroom? How can you encourage learners to understand their own learning, as a means to motivate them further? You need to think about how and when you can provide opportunities for learners to articulate their own learning and strategies for learning. Do not get distracted by the need to 'deliver subject content'. The process and skill of thinking is, perhaps, more important to learning than the actual content of the substantive curriculum the learner is following at any given moment.

Idea 12.1

Going meta

Pose challenging questions to learners to help them really engage with why they do the things they do and have the answers they have. Get them to reflect upon their own work, answers and learning as a means to stretch them further.
    Always ask:

- Why do you think that?
- How did you come to that answer?
- Is there another way you might do it?
- Before you do this, what do you think the outcome/result will be? Why?

 Idea 12.2

Unlocking attitudes

The starting point for thinking about thinking is to explore with learners what their pre-existing attitudes are to thinking – how they see thinking working and what approaches they think they take, and what difficulties they have. Get learners to explore 'learning conversations' where they reflect, list in a written form and share with peers what they think thinking is. This provides you with an avenue to explore with them strategies they might adopt from each other and to raise the issue of thinking so that you can open the way into explaining the use of the other ideas in this chapter.

 Idea 12.3

If . . . then . . . but . . .

When learners are planning and doing project work get them to explore the consequences and likely outcomes of problems in advance of coming across them. Get them to make flow charts or maps where they say to themselves:

- If I do this . . .
- Then this might happen . . .

(Continued)

(Continued)

- But if this happens, I could . . ..
- However, then this might happen instead . . .
- Then I could . . .

In this example, you are able to stretch learners and ask them to predict outcomes and consequences of decisions before they start work on problems or projects.

Idea 12.4

Get vocal

An essential component in meta-cognition is to get learners to explain their own thinking – to themselves and to others. They need to be able to be given opportunities to say and document/record how they are going about the process of their thinking. They also then need to have opportunities to reflect upon their own thinking, shedding further light on their own understanding of what they are doing.

To do this you could set aside formal class time on a regular basis – maybe at the end of projects or assignments (or at a mid-point) and ask learners to record the processes they are using and the steps they are taking. This 'reflective time' could enable them to have the chance – structured into lessons – to share thinking strategies and to reflect upon how else they might go about their work, and their responses to it.

Idea 12.5

Why? Because?

This activity is something you can do through questioning techniques or through structured group work. It is a way of extending and challenging learners. Ask them 'Why?' to a statement they have made – maybe a low-level factual statement from your subject area. They have to reply with a sentence which starts 'Because . . .'. You can keep this going for a while and really build upon learning, making the learning deeper the more you extend the questioning.

Idea 12.6

Ranking and categorizing

Encourage learners to put ideas, theories, case studies, examples and other substantive content from your subject specialism and curriculum into lists, ordering and re-ordering them from 'most true' down to 'least true' in a hierarchy. Get them to start to make choices over what they think is true, useful, least useful and most contested. This would be an ideal exercise to be completed collaboratively – and always generates debate and discussion. The 'learning', so to speak, is not necessarily in the final answer but, rather, in the process and negotiation undertaken to complete the exercise.

 Idea 12.7

You are always on my mind

Encourage learners to present their thoughts about a topic in a visual way on a regular basis. Use word clouds from websites such as Wordle.com, MindMaps, word lists, and so on, and provide regular opportunities for learners to 'summarize where they are' and what they can remember. It is important for their own reflection that they get used to thinking 'What do I know?' all the way through their learning. This makes an ideal starter or end activity for a lesson. These could be used to make revision posters for learners to display around the teaching space or even in their own private study space at home.

 Idea 12.8

Top Trumps

Do you remember the game Top Trumps? You would buy a pack of playing cards on a theme which would have a picture and then a list of categories/powers. You and a friend would choose a card in secret, agree a category and then decide which card had the 'best' or 'highest' rating/ranking for that category. The winner keeps the card of the other player and then chooses again. You carry on until all the cards have been won by one of the players.

Why not get learners to make their own top trump card decks based around a topic from your substantive curriculum content. They would need to design the artwork, set the categories and make the pictures. The learning here is in the processes of synthesis and evaluation needed to categorize and rank the objects of the knowledge.

Idea 12.9

Sequencing

A key aspect of meta-cognitive thinking is the role played by 'sequencing' in thinking. In other words, the ability to order things into start/middle/end enables the learner/thinker to look over and above the individual bits of knowledge and look more at the process and connections between them. In a very simplistic (but highly effectively) way sequencing things into a narrative order helps learners to do this, and deepens understanding. Cut out lots of statements about your subject matter which might relate to each other in sequences of twos, threes, fours, and so on. Ask learners to find the connected statements and then sequence each set. You can make the sequences and matching sets as complex as you feel the learners need.

Thinking and thinking skills

Adey et al. (1999), in contrast to dominant models of 'learning styles' (for example, the visual auditory kinaesthetic (VAK) system), argue that teachers and learners need to think about learning 'strategies', rather than 'styles' as means to support learners' learning and thinking at deeper levels. They suggest that a learning strategy is a collection of skills and approaches that learners use, together, to help them make sense of and complete tasks. In thinking about strategies in this way, we are not saying that thinking approaches are 'fixed' or are biologically determined (as is believed within some of the 'learning styles' debates). Rather, we learn how to learn. It is an active process, which we can practise and get better at.

 Reflection point

Can thinking be taught? For Adey et al. (1999) teachers can help equip learners with a 'toolbox' of approaches and techniques that they can use to develop their learning strategies. This means how we learn can be developed and can change over time and according to the nature of the task and problem we are learning. The key development in learning how to learn is that learners can make informed choices over the selection of the learning strategies they choose when confronted with something new. The role of the teacher, then, is to provide access to a wide range of approaches to thinking, helping learners to build their toolboxes in much the same way that this book helps the teacher build theirs.

Best practice – the 'thinking literature'

Although the literature on thinking is confused and contradictory, there are some important key messages:

- Open tasks often encourage creativity.
- Socratic questions (see Chapter 11) can stretch and challenge learners.
- Learners need to manipulate old and new knowledge together and find ways to connect it together.
- Meta-cognition is essential in developing thinking skills and processes further.
- Learners need to have opportunities to articulate their thinking – and to articulate how they go about their thinking.
- Getting learners to 'think' and to challenge their thinking at the start of lessons draws them in and develops interesting and exciting lessons.
- If learners feel they are thinking and can see the benefits then this is highly motivating.

 Idea 12.10

Put your hat on . . .

This idea draws upon the 'six thinking hats' method developed by Edward De Bono (1985) in his book of the same name. Each 'hat' is a way to look at and think about a problem, drawing upon a different skills-set or perspective. In the words of De Bono, the hats are:

- White hat – 'facts and figures'
- Red hat – 'emotions and feelings'
- Black hat – 'cautious and careful'
- Yellow hat – 'speculative-positive'
- Green hat – 'creative thinking'.
- Blue hat – 'control of thinking'.

In other words,

1. White hat – used for neutral thinking where you only state facts and ignore everything else other than what is known/proven.
2. Red hat – the wearer of the red hat can only discuss how the issue being looked at makes them feel.

(Continued)

(Continued)

3. Black hat – used for highlighting problems – 'negative thinking' – always listing warnings or predicting risks.
4. Yellow hat – used for 'pie in the sky' thinking; only looking at the positives – only stating possibilities and looking at speculating positive outcomes and benefits.
5. Green hat – used for really trying to innovate – thinking 'outside of the box' – coming up with unusual and unpredictable ideas.
6. Blue hat – used for meta-cognition. This is often seen as the 'control' hat as it thinks about all the other thinking done by all the other hats. It decides if the collective thinking of all the hats is moving on track or not.

De Bono says, 'The biggest enemy of thinking is complexity, for that leads to confusion. When thinking is clear and simple, it becomes more enjoyable and effective' (De Bono, 1985: 176). The idea is that if you adopt one hat, then you can think about a problem or task in a particular and focused way – avoiding confusion. You can then swap hats and think about the same problem in a different way, extending your thinking as you do so. Learners could do this for a problem using one hat at a time, or could be given hats individually, each contributing to group debates from a different perspective. This idea has many practical classroom and group-work applications, as the ideas below illustrate.

Idea 12.11

Six-way group planning

Organize groups so they have six members. Give each learner a different hat and ask them to debate an issue or plan a task/project. Each learner can only think through the perspective of the hat they are given. Record answers with a scribe – the blue hat might be best to do this in its 'overview' and reflective role.

Idea 12.12

Six-way jigsawing

Organize learners into groups of six. Each group has one of the different six hats. Once they have debated/worked on a planning task then jigsaw the groups (see Chapter 4), and re-combine the six groups so that they now comprise all six different hats. They then re-work the planning/problem combining all their different perspectives as they do so.

Best practice – making thinking fun!

One of the outcomes of using De Bono's six thinking hats is that thinking becomes quite fun. Learners really respond well to the framework of having a hat to think through; it provides just enough structure and framework to allow for clarity and avoid complication and yet it does provide a genuine challenge. Think about the following if you intend to adopt this thinking strategy in your classes:

- Buy different coloured hats for learners.
- Ask learners to make their own hats.
- Place hats on tables so learners have a visual representation of what group they are in.
- Swap roles/hats between learners often, to create variety.
- Always remember to 'pull together' the different forms of thinking at the end of the exercise. Work of this nature really raises the importance of plenaries in lessons (see Chapter 5) to ensure that all the loose strands can be tied up.

 Reflection point

The six thinking hats method does not just work for learners! You could try this in planning meetings with colleagues. Maybe you can try and use the strategy with colleagues for planning before you then try it out with learners; it might help you to clarify your own understanding of the hats and to raise possible points of confusion and alert you to problems before you try it for real.

 Idea 12.13

'Concept mapping'

Following on from Ideas 3.8 and 12.7, Adey et al. (1999) refer to the importance of 'concept mapping' as a key learning strategy for helping learners to explore and expand their thinking. The idea is simple – to encourage deeper learning and higher-order thinking, learners need to be encouraged to see the connections between things. Equally, making connections – inventing new connections – is itself a higher-level form of thinking as it encourages manipulation of 'raw knowledge' into a new product.

Time should therefore be spent encouraging learners to connect and link ideas, terms, modules, case studies, and so on from your subject matter as a means to develop their abilities to synthesize.

Best practice – building a 'thinking classroom'

McGregor (2007) identifies a range of strategies that teachers can adopt to build thinking more strongly into their classrooms:

- Ask interesting questions at the start of the lesson to arouse curiosity.
- Encourage learners to adopt the opposite view to what they actually think when discussing ideas in class. This is sometimes called encouraging 'cognitive conflict'.
- Encourage learners to be reflective – to think about how they go about tasks and problems.
- Always try to encourage learners to find the means to articulate why they think as they do.
- Always use collaborative learning strategies whereby learners can be exposed to the thinking of others.

Best practice – reflecting upon learning

Much of the literature referenced in this chapter notes the importance of getting learners to think about their thinking and the processes they go through. How often do we, as teachers, really talk to our learners about what learning is and how it works? This is, after all, the whole basis for the relationships and social encounters we have with them. It is recommended that you:

1. Explore with learners what they think thinking is; get them excited about your own 'thinking classroom'.
2. Encourage learners to describe what they think learning is; share your own views of what learning is and how it works. This will develop insightful conversational relationships with your learners and it is an excellent way to demonstrate what your expectations are of them.
3. Use the conversations above as a means to 'hook' learners into why you ask them to do the task they do. Justify to your learners why they are going to experience lessons in the way you have planned. This is highly motivating for learners to 'see the point' behind teacher decision-making (see Chapter 8).

Questions for professional development

1. Do you allow enough time for learners to think about their thinking? How can you structure this time into the usual lesson routine?

2. What learning strategies are your learners adopting? Get them to articulate these as a means to encourage their reflection.
3. What are your own assumptions about what learning is and how it works? Why do you plan for the tasks that you do? How does your pedagogy match what you think about the learning process?
4. Teachers are learners too! Do you learn through reflection? If so, how might this benefit your own learners?

Checklist: building your toolbox

- Build excitement about 'thinking' among your class.
- Challenge and probe with interesting and stimulating questions at the start of the lesson.
- Build-in opportunities for learners to map and draw what they know and the connections between bits of curriculum content and knowledge.
- Be open with learners about the need to understand their own thinking better.
- Adopt labelling, sequencing and mapping activities which help learners develop connections between things.

Chapter links

The ideas in this chapter relate closely to those also explored in Chapters 6, 11 and 13.

Further reading

De Bono, E. (1985) *Six Thinking Hats*. London: Penguin.
A really easy to read exploration of the nature and complexity of thinking and how we might make our thinking clearer and less complicated.

McGuiness, C. (1999) *From Thinking Skills to Thinking Classrooms*. London: DfEE.
A very useful overview of the field of 'thinking skills' from a leading report in the 'thinking skills movement'.

CHAPTER 13

CAPTURING AND UTILIZING THE LEARNER VOICE

Chapter overview

The aims of the chapter are to:

1. Demonstrate the links between listening to and using the learner voice and motivation.
2. Provide practical examples for how to incorporate the learner voice into your classroom teaching.
3. Illustrate the role that emergent technologies can play in utilizing learner voice.
4. Provide ideas for learner engagement and involvement based upon meta-cognitive opportunities.

Problem-solving

There is a growing body of literature that suggests that there are some profound links between 'learner voice' and motivation. The idea, put simply, is that listening to learners and responding seriously to their feedback gives them an increased sense of both their own worth and that of their learning

(Assessment Reform Group, 2002). For many practitioners, however, creative use of the learner voice is challenging. If the learner voice is not followed up then these attempts look cynical and worthless. However, finding exciting means to keep learners motivated beyond the 'usual routine' of evaluation questionnaires at the end of the term is time-consuming. It could be the case, then, that capturing learner voice and not being seen to follow this up could be more demotivating that not capturing it in the first place.

Teaching and learning do not, somehow, happen in 'isolation' from the learners; good teaching involves learners at every stage that it is appropriate to do so. Good teachers are able to build the rapport and learning atmosphere needed to be relatively open with learners about the teaching and learning that takes place. In turn, being seen to capture and utilize learner voice and opinions develops further productive learning atmospheres. It focuses the group around their collective self-interest, the very prime point of their social relationship.

In this final chapter we discuss many simple ideas for classroom teachers to adopt when seeking to elicit evaluation from their learners. These ideas should enable teachers to obtain extremely valuable evaluation of teaching and learning strategies, while at the same time enabling learners to feel both involved and valued in the process of their own learning. In many cases they also offer opportunities for learners to reflect upon the nature of their own learning, and 'learn about their own learning' – what we call 'meta-cognition' (see Chapter 12 for an extended discussion).

Context

In discussing the concept 'motivation to learn' the Assessment Reform Group (2002) draw upon findings from Harlen and Deakin Crick (2002). For learners to develop the 'motivation to learn' they need to feel that they have control over aspects of their own learning and understand how to exercise control over their own skills and self-efficacy. We might refer to this as their 'locus of control' – how much learners feel in control of their own learning. Capturing their views and opinions, providing opportunities for reflection and open debate, and utilizing peer support are all ways in which teachers can structure into their teaching the means to help learners understand and extend their own loci of control. In discussing the notion of an 'active citizenship' in UK schools a number of commentators (such as Rudduck and Flutter, 2000) suggest that in order to develop learners who can participate in society in a socially responsible fashion we need to involve them in decision-making. Allowing young people to have a voice is a means of educating them about their own role in the world, as much as it is about their own role in their classes and their learning.

Capturing learner voice, however, is by no means simple. The whole use of such data comes with a warning (Fielding, 2004; Rudduck and McIntyre, 2007); namely that cynical attempts to capture learner voice for performativity purposes alone end up perpetuating the cynical use of learners as 'objects' passive in their own education journeys. If you seek to motivate your learners by involving them further in their learning, then do so motivated by a genuine attempt to engage and involve young people in their own active citizenship and awareness of their learning about their learning. You must also be prepared to hear things that you do not like, and will need to deal with these as genuinely as possible.

Toolbox

The role of student evaluation in teaching and learning

Learner voice has both 'macro' and 'micro' components: learner voice capture and utilization can be used across the whole of your institution as a means to enhance the learning atmosphere and ethos of the institution as a whole; learner voice can be captured by individual teachers as a reflection of their individual classrooms and as a means to motivate and engage small groups. The following suggestions provide some ideas for how classroom teachers can add such strategies to their classroom repertoire.

Best practice – listening to learners? What is in it for us?

In the QCA briefing paper *Pupil Voice is Here to Stay!* Jean Rudduck (2005) outlined the benefits of using learner voice – for both schools/colleges and for the learners themselves. It can be summarized as:

- Learner voice can offer a meaningful basis for genuine partnership between teachers and learners.
- It can produce a practical agenda for change.
- Change can be 'owned' by all.
- Learners can feel included and involved – they can feel a sense of 'agency'.

- Educational institutions can become more inclusive of the wide diversity of interests and 'voices' on offer.
- With the feeling they belong, comes the opportunity for learners to feel they own the future direction of their own learning.

Listening to learners, therefore, can motivate teachers as much as it can motivate learners.

Idea 13.1

Routine ends to lessons

There is something to be said for your capture of the learner voice to be unusual and varied. Sometimes routine and pattern create a sameness which does not have quite the same 'motivational spark' as an unusual or unexpected strategy does. Having said this, something familiar about routines often – over a period of time – reaps deeper rewards in terms of the richness of the information you can glean, and the relationship you can bound with your learners. A really simple suggestion for a routine that you can build into your classes is to ask learners to make a note of what they have learnt in each session. Alternatively they might tell you what has been successful and what they feel they need to do more of or differently. Keep these and then respond to them in your planning. Make sure learners see the connections between what you are asking them, what they are telling you and what happens in the teaching–learning relationship.

Idea 13.2

Well done! What next . . .?

This is both an unusual mechanism for rewarding and praising learners, and a means to follow this up with a small piece of evaluation. Produce glossy, well-constructed postcards with a 'Well done' message that the teacher can then add to and personalize. You might congratulate a learner on a particular piece of work or on a presentation and so on. These postcards can be distributed through tutor groups or maybe even posted home. Along with the 'Well done' postcard you can include a 'Tell us about' postcard. In this, the learner provides one positive about their teaching and learning experience, a couple of ideas for improvement and a self-assessment of what they think their next learning challenge will be. In this way the praise and the reward lead to a continued conversation, albeit at a distance.

Reflection point

This chapter – and indeed this book as a whole – looks at issues of motivation and engagement within individual classrooms. But this is not the end of the story – and this is especially true for issues of learner voice. How many of the ideas herein can be used across your wider institution? Are there ideas and strategies here that might work better as team solutions? It is true to say that the sum is greater than the individual parts. If lots of different colleagues all captured learner voice in a variety of ways, and then used this data to compare and discuss, then across the institution learners would feel more motivated, more quickly.

 Idea 13.3

Peer video

Video older learners talking about the work your current learners are undertaking. Elicit from the older students top tips and advice; ask them to make personal and individual comments about the subject matter and what they feel about it. Show these recordings to younger groups as a means to stimulate their own discussions. Get them to have an opinion about their learning, what they are learning, and about how they are best learning it. Show that it is important to have a view about your learning, rather than see it as something that 'happens to you'.

Idea 13.4

Organize 'induction' talks

At key points in your teaching – induction weeks, new terms, new topics and so on – invite into your class older learners to speak about the topic/project/year ahead. Show your learners it is important to think about what they are doing and to openly discuss expectations and desires. Encourage them to tell you what they like and want to get out of topics/subjects/curriculum areas.

Idea 13.5

Use choice as a means to respond to learner feedback

It is really vital that, after having asked learners what they think and need from you, that you respond – and are seen to respond. You could plan teaching sessions where, in groups, learners have a choice over the activity they do, the way they complete a task, or the difficulty and challenge of the task they do. Show them that the choices on offer come directly from the things they have said to you that they like or need more help with, or find most effective.

 Idea 13.6

Thumbs up and thumbs down

You could make cards with a hand and 'thumbs up' picture on it. Alternatively, learners could draw their own, or even photograph their own hands and print these onto cardboard or index cards.

   At key points in the lesson, the teacher can ask students if they understand, or if they need more time or can complete the task in the original time offered. At each of these points, learners can show a 'thumbs up' or 'thumbs down' sign as their 'vote', and can do this relatively comfortably as part of a whole-class answer. The teacher can then respond accordingly.

Listening to learners

To make truly meaningful your capture of the learners' voice – you need to listen to what they have to say. This is an important point. The purpose of the exercise is not to simply produce 'data' but to actually connect with learners – and get learners to connect with their own learning and to each other.

 Idea 13.7

Personalize learning and personalize wall displays

Ask learners to tell you, as a bite-sized written statement, what the subject they are studying 'means to them'. Alternatively, you could ask them what the most interesting aspect of the subject/topic is, or what they like most about the lessons. Type up

(Continued)

(Continued)

these quotations and turn them into a poster with a head and shoulders picture of the learner (with suitable approval and permissions). These posters can be copied onto a range of different-coloured cards and laminated for future use. They would make an excellent wall display in a classroom and an engaging display for parents' evenings and open evenings. They would be a fun and simple way to demonstrate what learners have to say and how they feel about their learning in your subject.

Idea 13.8

Spoken word 1 – podcasting the learner

There is something about the richness of the spoken word that really adds a layer of depth and authenticity to what learners have to say, if you can capture them talking. Digital voice records that record near-perfect sound quality in industry-standard MP3 format are relatively cheap and easily accessible. It would be a good idea to record learners talking about their lessons – how they are taught, what they find most interesting and what the greatest challenges are. These sound files (with appropriate permissions and anonymities, if needed) could then be put on websites or into virtual learning environments (VLEs) for new learners to access and listen to – maybe within the first few weeks of a class.

Idea 13.9

Spoken word 2 – FAQs

Following on from Idea 13.8, you could encourage learners to record answers to all the frequently asked questions (FAQs) that are usually asked about your lessons/subjects. These could then be posted on VLEs or as part of your institution's library pages. They could also be made into a 'sound display' for prospective parents and learners at welcome evenings and open-day/evening events.

Idea 13.10

Spoken word 3 – record book reviews

Using the digital voice recording technology highlighted in Ideas 13.8 and 13.9, you could ask learners to undertake book reviews/summaries and post these onto the VLE or your library's web pages. These audio reviews could also be flagged-up on the library's book stock – maybe with a little card on the shelves indicating where a student review is accessible for a given book. Learners can then listen to the review/summary and make up their own minds.

Best practice – using audio to capture the learner voice

When making audio recordings of learners – as we quite literally capture the learner 'voice' – it is helpful to consider the following:

- Purchase a digital voice recorder that records in MP3 format. Once you own one of these you will find many educational uses for it (see Chapter 7 for ideas on the use of e-learning to engage learners).
- Record in MP3 format so that the majority of your audience will be able to play back the file without any difficulty.
- Find a quiet room, as background noise can ruin the best intended recordings.
- Always talk learners through what will happen with the audio files afterwards – ensure that learners sign to give permission to release the file to you.
- Leave a little pause between starting the recording and asking the learner to speak ('cue' them in with a gesture). This will help if you need to edit the file afterwards.
- If you need to cut a little bit off the end of the recording, or turn a long recording into two separate, shorter pieces, you can use a variety of simple to use, and often free, software to edit your audio files (and that you have permission to edit). A popular software is Audacity (located at: http://audacity.source forge.net/) although you would need to seek permission from your IT and network support staff before downloading and using this.
- Try and keep the length of recordings down: smaller files often make the point much 'punchier'.
- You might wish to offer to give the learners a copy of the recording as a small 'thank you' for taking part.

∿ Reflection point

Are there ways you can use audio recordings of learners as the basis for a team or staff project? Can learner recordings be a useful stimulus/resource for CPD activities based upon evaluation of the teaching and learning provision?

Idea 13.11

Tweet tweet

This idea comes from the work of Martin Waller (2010), a primary practitioner in Stockton, UK. In exploring literacies among his primary class, he adopted the social networking platform Twitter as a means to provide a vehicle/forum through which learners can share their learning with an outside audience. This is integrated into the normal, everyday routines of the classroom. A networked PC is set up with an open Twitter stream. Learners are able to articulate in 'Tweets' what they are doing, what they think has value and what they feel they are learning. The Twitter account is protected so that the member of staff manages who gets to see the Tweets and who might Tweet back. In exploring their learning in this way, learners are able to both own the learning and feel it is of value to express an opinion on learning as a process in general. Although this is an example from the primary sector in the UK, it is possible to see how this can be adopted by other practitioners in exciting ways. The idea of having a learner Tweet adding a meta-conversational element to what goes on in the classroom as a 'live' and normal part of the lesson's routine is really exciting, although such an idea needs some very careful planning and 'rule-setting' with those who use it to ensure it is successful and appropriate.

Further information about this project can be obtained on the website: http://www.changinghorizons.net/

Reflection point

The use of e-learning tools and technologies is often considered to lead, if used successfully, to increased levels of engagement as they both offer a rich and interactive experience which learners can access outside of school/college and, depending on the resource, in their own time. See Chapter 7 for a fuller discussion of this. Consider here how you might adopt technology to capture aspects of the teaching and learning process and learners' evaluation and review of it. Can you use email or send messages within a VLE as a means for learners to post ideas and suggestions to you? Can you set up a discussion forum once a term, within your VLE, where your classes post comments on their own learning and which aspects of the teaching most help them?

Idea 13.12
Identifying trouble hot spots

As teachers we sometimes do not recognize that some learners often feel threatened in various parts of the institution, for example, on staircases, in the toilets. Get students in pairs to draw diagrams of the school/college/immediate local area and identify areas they feel 'safe' or 'unsafe'. You can then feed these ideas back to your team/department/management team in response to students' concerns about particular trouble hot spots.

Best practice – students as researchers

There is a movement within learner voice practices to use learners themselves as 'researchers' in their own educational and institutional settings (see Fielding and Bragg, 2003). Many practitioners – and wider, whole institutions – find this an extremely exciting and worthwhile aspect of the learner voice agenda. They feel that the quality and depth of the learner engagement and involvement, the skills they develop and the quality of information produced are often outstanding. If you are thinking of an approach such as this, consider the following:

- How will you recruit the learners? What skills do they need to already have? What skills will participation in the activity build for them?
- How will you train these young people to be 'researchers'? Can you explore links with local universities in order to do this? Schools of social science and education might have specialist support and training on offer – it would certainly make an interesting basis for partnership and might add an extra motivational layer for the young people involved and their aspirations if they can have support from university teachers or older students.
- What methods to capture data would the young researchers adopt? How will they record the data and write it up?
- What support will the institution give these young people to do this work and where does the extra time (both staff and learners') come from?

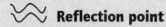 **Reflection point**

Could student research form the basis for internal/whole institutional reviews? Could a team of learners produce a report for staff, parents and governors on their findings? Could you publish it and encourage a wider, outside audience to come and hear about the project and the data that the young people produced?

Questions for professional development

1. What mechanisms work best for you and your learners? Are there any strategies that are so effective that you are incorporating them into your usual routine?
2. Do you have the technological resources to post and upload video clips, audio files and host chats? Do you and your colleagues need further training in these aspects of e-learning?
3. How can you show learners that their opinion matters? How can you demonstrate to them the impact and legacy of the things you ask and the things they say to you?
4. After using learner voice strategies for some time, are you able to see changes in class ethos and atmosphere or your relationships with groups and specific learners? Are these worth forming the basis of professional conversations with colleagues? What do you have to disseminate to them that is of value? What insights do you now have to share?

Checklist: building your toolbox

- Use both varied routine and strategies but also bed down simple mechanisms to capture learner voice all the way through your teaching.
- Try to use digital technologies as a means to capture what students are saying.
- Always listen to what they are saying and respond accordingly – do not keep your response secret, show them how their voice matters and leads to change.
- Be prepared to hear what you might not wish to! Otherwise the purpose is unauthentic and meaningless.
- Capture audios, quotations, comments and use these for induction, open evenings and parents' evenings.

- Personalize your teaching room and spaces with learner quotes and posters.
- Build learners' opinions and ideas about your subject into your teaching – use audio reviews, video presentations, and so on – as a means to encourage general further discussion between and within class groupings.

Chapter links

The ideas in this chapter relate closely with those also explored in Chapters 4, 5, 7 and 12.

Further reading

Fielding, M. and Bragg, S. (2003) *Students as Researchers: Making a Difference*. Cambridge: Pearson.
An excellent overview of the practicalities and benefits of encouraging students to investigate their own educational institutions.

REFERENCES

Adey, P., Fairbrother, R. and Wiliam, D., with Johnson, B. and Jones, C. (1999) *Learning Styles and Strategies: A Review of Research*. London: Ofsted/Kings College, London School of Economics.

Anderson, L.W., Krathwohl, D. (eds) (2001) *A Taxonomy for Learning, Teaching and Assessing: A Revision of Bloom's Taxonomy of Educational Objectives*. New York: Longman.

Aronson, E., Bridgeman, D.L. and Geffner, R. (1978) 'Interdependent interactions and prosocial behavior', *Journal of Research and Development in Education*, 12: 16–26.

Assessment Reform Group (1999) *Assessment for Learning: Beyond the Black Box*. Cambridge: University of Cambridge School of Education.

Assessment Reform Group (2002) *Testing, Motivating and Learning*. Cambridge: University of Cambridge.

Bandler, R. and Grinder, J. (1981) *Reframing: Neuro-Linguistic Programming and the Transformation of Meaning*. Colorado: Real People Press.

Bandura, A. (2006) 'Toward a psychology of human agency', *Perspectives on Psychological Science*, 1(2): 164–80.

Bennett, S., Maton, K. and Kervin, L. (2008) 'The digital natives debate: a critical review of the evidence', *British Journal of Educational Technology*, 39(5): 775–86.

Black, P. and Wiliam, D. (1998) *Inside the Black Box: Raising Standards through Classroom Assessment*. London: NferNelson.

Black, P., Harison, C., Lee, C., Marshall, B. and Wiliam, D. (2003) *Assessment for Learning: Putting it into Practice*. Maidenhead: Open University Press.

Bloom, B.S. (1956a) *Taxonomy of Educational Objectives, Handbook I: The Cognitive Domain*. New York: David McKay.

Bloom, B.S. (1956b) *Taxonomy of Educational Objectives: The Classification of Educational Goals*. New York: Susan Fauer.

Bonk, C. and Graham, C. (2005) *The Handbook of Blended Learning*. Pfeiffer Wiley.

Chi-Kin Lee, J., Hongbiao, Y. and Zhang, Z. (2009) 'Exploring the influence of the classroom environment on students motivation and self-regulated learning in Hong Kong'. *The Asia-Pacific Educational Researcher*, 18(2): 219–32.

De Bono, E. (1985) *Six Thinking Hats*. London: Penguin.

Department for Children, Schools and Families (DCSF) (2008) *Safer Children in a Digital World. The Report of the Byron Review*. Crown Copyright. Nottingham: DCSF Publications.

Duncan, T.G. and McKeachie, W.J. (2005) 'The making of the motivated strategies for learning questionnaire', *Educational Psychologist*, 40(2): 117–28.

Epstein, J.L. (1988) 'Homework practices, achievements and behaviors of elementary school students', *Personality and Social Psychology Bulletin*, 21: 215–25.

Fielding, M. (2004) 'Transformative approaches to student voice: theoretical underpinnings, recalcitrant realities', *British Educational Research Journal*, 30(2): 295–311.

Fielding, M. and Bragg, S. (2003) *Students as Researchers: Making a Difference*. Cambridge: Pearson.

Fishbein, M. and Ajzen, I. (1975) *Belief, Attitude, Intention, and Behavior: An Introduction to Theory and Research*. Reading, MA: Addison-Wesley.

Galton, M., Steward, S., Hargreaves, L., Page, C. and Pell, A. (2009) *Motivating your Secondary Class*. London: Sage.

Gardner, H. (1993) *Frames of Mind: The Theory of Multiple Intelligences*. New York: Basic Books.

General Teaching Council (GTC) (2008) 'Research for teachers: strategies for supporting dyslexic pupils' available from: www.gtce.org.uk

Gilbert, I. (2002) *Essential Motivation in the Classroom*. London: Routledge/Falmer.

Hallam, S. (2000) *Homework: The Evidence*. London: Institute of Education, University of London.

Hanrahan, M. (1998) 'The effect of learning environment factors on students' motivation and learning', *International Journal of Science Education*, 20(6): 737–53.

Harlen, W. and Deakin Crick, R. (2002) 'A systematic review of the impact of summative assessment and tests on pupils' motivation for learning (EPPI-Centre Review)', in *Research Evidence in Education Library*, issue 1. London: EPPI-Centre, Social Science Research Unit, Institute of Education.

Hay McBer (2000) *Research into Teacher Effectiveness: A Model of Teacher Effectiveness*, report by Hay McBer to the Department for Education and Employment, June. London: DfEE.

Joint Information Systems Committee (JISC) (2007) *In Their Own Words: Exploring the Learners' Perspective on E-Learning*. London: JISC.

Kidd, W. and Czerniawski, G. (2010) *Successful Teaching 14–19: Theory, Practice and Reflection*. London: Sage.

Marland, M. (1993) *The Craft of the Classroom*. London: Heinemann.

Maslow, A. (1987) *Motivation and Personality*. New York: Harper and Row.

McGregor, D. (2007) *Developing Thinking, Developing Learning: A Guide to Thinking Skills in Education*. Maidenhead: Open University Press.

McGuiness, C. (1999) *From Thinking Skills to Thinking Classrooms*. London: DfEE.

Prensky, M. (2001) 'Digital natives, digital immigrants', *On the Horizon*, 9(5). MCB University Press.

Muijs, D. and Reynolds, D. (2010) *Effective Teaching: Evidence and Practice*, 3rd edn. London: Sage.

Piaget, J. (1950) *The Psychology of Intelligence*. New York: Routledge.

Reiss, S. (2000) *Who Am I: The 16 Basic Desires that Motivate Our Actions and Define Our Personalities*. New York: Tarcher/Putnam.

Richardson, W. (2010) *Blogs, Wikis, Podcasts and Other Powerful Web Tools for Classrooms*, 3rd edn. Thousand Oaks, CA: Corwin.

Rogers, B. (1998) *You Know the Fair Rule: Strategies for Making the Hard Job of Discipline and Behavior Management in School Easier*, 2nd edn. London: Prentice Hall.

Rogers, B. (2011) *Classroom Behaviour: A Practical Guide to Effective Teaching, Behaviour Management and Colleague Support*, 3rd edn. London: Sage.

Rosenberg, M. (2001) *E-Learning: Strategies for Delivering Knowledge in the Digital Age*. New York: McGraw-Hill.

Rudduck, J. (2005) *Pupil Voice is Here to Stay*. London: QCA. http://www.service schoolsmobilitytoolkit.com/resourcedownloads/staffroom/bpv_theneedtoinvolve pupilvoice.pdf; http://www.ttrb.ac.uk/ViewArticle.aspx?contentId=13008

Rudduck, J. and Flutter, J. (2000) 'Pupil participation and the pupil perspective: carving a new order of experience', *Cambridge Journal of Education*, 30(1): 75–89.

Rudduck, J. and McIntyre, D. (ed.) (2007) *Improving Learning Through Consulting Pupils. Teaching and Learning Research Programme (TLRP) Consulting Pupils Project Team*. London: Routledge.

Salmon, G., Edirisingha, P., Mobbs, M., Mobbs, R. and Dennett, C. (2008) *How to Create Podcasts for Education*. Maidenhead: Open University Press/McGraw Hill.

Savill-Smith, C., Attewell, J. and Stead, G. (2006) *Mobile Learning in Practice: Piloting a Mobile Learning Teachers' Toolkit in Further Education Colleges*. https://crm. isnlearning.org.uk/user/login.aspx?code=062526&P=062526PD&action=pdfdl& src=XOWEB

Soloman, Y., Warin, J. and Lewis, C. (2002) Helping with homework? Homework as a site of tension for parents and teenagers, *British Educational Research Journal*, 28(4): 603–22.

Stephenson, J. (ed.) (2001) *Teaching and Learning Online: Pedagogies for New Technologies*. London: Kogan Page.

Stern, J. (2009) *Getting the Buggers to do their Homework*, 2nd edn. London: Continuum.

Waller, M. (2010) '"It's very very fun and ecsiting" – using Twitter in the primary classroom', *English Four to Eleven*, Summer(39): 14–16.

Walker, J.M.T. and Hoover-Dempsey, K.V. (2001) Age-related patterns in student invitations to parental involvement in homework. Paper presented at the Annual Meeting of the American Educational Research Association, San Diego, CA.

Wenger, R. (1998) *Communities of Practice: Learning, Meaning and Identity*. Cambridge: Cambridge University Press.

Wertsch, J.V. (1997) *Vygotsky and the Formation of the Mind*. Cambridge, MA: Harvard University Press.

YPeer (2005) *The Youth Peer Education Tool Kit – The Training of Trainers' Manual*. New York: The Youth Peer Education and Training Network.

INDEX

Added to a page number 'f' denotes a figure.